STRAINING AT THE OARS

LEWIS R. SHELTON

DEDICATION

Though many people undoubtedly deserve
special recognition in the publication of my first book,
my parents and the parents of my wife, Margaret,
truly contributed more than an attempted
description can afford.
Therefore, I dedicate this book in loving memory to
James and Rosalie Shelton and
Paul and Nona Hill.

TABLE OF CONTENTS

ACKNOWLEDGMENTS

First, I must acknowledge and thank my
wife of more than 50 years for her incredible
faith, support, and encouragement.

Second, my children and grandchildren have
read and reread, questioned and made
suggestions, all leading to a completed work.

My granddaughter, Maggie Shader, deserves
special thanks for her creation of the cover.

Finally, I express my appreciation and recognition to
Susan Meamber, my editor extraordinaire.

INTRODUCTION

Over the course of my life and ministry, I have learned many lessons. Undoubtedly, I missed a few critical educational experiences along the way—some because I wasn't ready or willing to embrace it at that particular juncture while others were simply missed opportunities. Yet, a commitment to honesty provokes confession. At times, I have been known to cruise mindlessly—day-dreaming my way into the future, invoking the "would-a, should-a, could-a" responses to any challenge posed against my conjured possibilities. However, the alarm clock of life prohibits prolonged seasons of inattentiveness, arresting consciousness, and capturing energies. Consequently, avoiding life's lessons may be more difficult than engaging them. With that said, I venture to share some of what I have learned, borrowing in the process from other people whom I admire, know, and/or respect. None of us live long enough to learn all we need to know via "the school of hard-knocks." Therefore, learning from other individuals provides what might be considered a graduate education at a fraction of the price.

Subscribing to the notion that this expression should be more than personal conjecture and opinion, we begin with a review of a favorite story out of the Gospels. This will provide a springboard from which to launch this project, while creating a touchstone to lend biblical credence to my suppositions. The Gospel account serves as one of the "ah-ha moments" in the lives of the disciples and stimulates contemplation and possible application for those following the same Shepherd, committed to the same Cause, and desiring to please the same Master.

CHAPTER 1

The Backdrop

As we begin, I must confess: I am a preacher. For some 50 years it has been my privilege and joy to serve as a minister. When I read a biblical story I not only seek to garner truth and application for my life, but strive to understand all I can for the sake of teaching others. Consequently, this may seem somewhat like a sermon or apologetic at first. Sorry, I can't help myself. However, it will not hurt, I promise. Climb in the boat and enjoy the ride. I will try to keep you from having to row.

Only a few dramatic moments in the life and ministry of Christ garner the attention of all four Gospel writers. One such event is the feeding of the 5,000 (Matthew 14:13-21; Mark 6:33-44; Luke 9:12-16; John 6:1-14). Leaders and preachers have effortlessly and frequently used this story, and it remains popular to this day. The compassion, power, and perspective of Jesus are all captured in the multiplication of a young man's lunch. Stomachs were filled while hearts were captivated and minds fascinated. This was no ordinary man; His words, as well as His manifestations, contradicted the possibility of that consideration. But who was He? Many people had this same question. The Twelve knew or, at least, we presume they knew. Jesus had been in a process of revealing himself to them, letting them know who He was and who His Father was, unveiling God's plans and purposes, and preparing them for their roles in the coming of His kingdom.

The story unfolds on the heels of news that John the Baptist had been beheaded by Herod. In a gesture to prove his power and impress his wife's daughter—who had impressed Herod and his guests with her dancing—the tetrarch agreed to a request for John's head. The young lady had been promised anything she wanted as a reward for her performance. One might think Herod happy to fulfill the desire since John had confronted him regarding the impropriety of stealing his brother Philip's wife. Yet, the Scripture states that Herod grieved over the request (Matthew 14:9). Herodias, however, had a grudge against John for his stance on the relationship she had with her "former" brother-in-law (Mark 6:19).

With the realization of this reality came the response of the Savior and His chosen. Recognizing His own sorrow, as well as the impact this cruel gesture had made on the Twelve, Jesus suggested that they withdraw from the crowds and the press of ministry. As they proceeded across the Sea of Galilee, news spread regarding their itinerary. People who desired to see and hear the Great Teacher (and possibly benefit from His miracles), left their homes and occupations to encounter Jesus upon His arrival. As frustrated as the disciples may have been, the Master felt nothing but compassion (Mark 6:34). Ministry was extended to those who had gathered, and soon the day came to a close. Jesus desired to provide them with an evening meal; the disciples desired to send them away to find their own provisions. Concluding that the treasury did not afford the capability of feeding the multitude, ostensibly a search for options began. Without further explanation, Andrew discovered a young man with five small loaves of bread and two fish. What followed defies explanation, outside of the miraculous.

Before considering the applicable lessons from this familiar Bible story, allow a somewhat off-centered, three-part parenthetical. First, people generally assume that the food contribution discovered by Andrew was the boy's lunch. Though possibly total conjecture, the thought remains, "Why did the lad still have that which had been provided for him with the day now nearing an end?" The text states:

> *"And when it was already quite late, His disciples came up to Him and began saying, 'The place is desolate and it is already quite late; send them away so that they may go into the surrounding countryside and villages and buy themselves something to eat.' But He answered and said to them, 'You give them something to eat!'"* (Mark 6:36, 37a)

One cannot determine the hour of the day from the simple description, but it would seem reasonable to conclude that hunger would be a common condition found within the multitude at that time of day. Nevertheless, the lad still had his lunch.

Having been a young man myself, I do not remember missing lunch very often, or any other meal for that matter. We were not flush, by any means. I grew up in a small lumber town in Northern California. My father worked for the mill as payroll master and personnel manager—not a bad position for one who only held a seventh grade education. My father was not paid well; his lack of education undoubtedly enabled the company to offer less than would seem appropriate. On top of this, my mother endured a number of maladies. I recall her experiencing fourteen operations during my childhood and adolescence. This added a serious financial burden on our family, since it was a number of years before my father was allowed to enjoy the insurance provided by the company because of his status as a white collar employee. My mother's previous medical history was also a factor, I'm sure. However, though finances were often tight, we always had something to eat. It wasn't fancy, but I never went hungry. Oh, there were times when I missed a meal, but that was because of my own choosing or lack of planning. For example, delighting in the opportunity for adventure, a fishing expedition might keep me away from home longer than had been originally planned. If the plan was for me to be away beyond meal time, my mom would have packed something for me to take along. Some times the level of fun I was experiencing trumped all other considerations: between the fishing and wading and playing and discovering, the day would slip away. In such cases, the lack of food did not compel us to go to the stores and restaurants within walking distance. As a norm, kids usually do not have any money; at least I can affirm that fact as a personal condition. Consequently, the remaining salmon eggs or wild berries found along the creek offered adequate provision for the moment. In other words, boys may miss their lunches, but usually that which is immediately available is seldom ignored. Therefore, I would suggest the first miracle in the story may well be the fact that the lad still had his lunch.

Second, it seems noteworthy to mention that apparently the young man gave what he had to Andrew. To picture the disciple wrestling to acquire the five loaves and two fish from the boy, as if he was reluctant to part with the same, seems a bit out of character for the disciples and would surely have been met with less than pleasure from the Lord. So, the boy gave what he had in spite of the fact that it was minuscule in the face of the need. I think this remains as an example for us today.

Third, when the disciples suggested that the crowd be sent away to find provisions, Jesus told them to provide what was needed: "You give them something to eat!" Without embellishing or adding unnecessary interpolation, there can be no doubt that our Lord speaks the same to His disciples today. Now, back to the story.

Organizing the crowd into groups of fifty people and inviting them to rest on the grassy shoreline, Jesus blessed the provision and broke it. He then distributed it to each of the disciples, who, in turn, gave a portion to each person present. We do not know how much they received, but we do know that they were satisfied. As the remnants were collected, a wave of adoration and recognition swept the crowd. This was no ordinary teacher of the Law—this was a prophet. Jesus, sensing their adulation, refused to simply allow their display of admiration and affirmation. To borrow from the Lord's words describing a somewhat similar opportunity, His attitude may well have been, *"My time is not yet at hand"* (John 7:6).[1] Desiring to spend time alone with the Father, three of the four Gospels[2] record that Jesus sent His disciples back across the Sea of Galilee, while He dismissed the multitude. The disciples, complying with the Master's wishes, began their journey across the same body of water they had traversed only hours earlier. They had made the initial trip anticipating rest and time to digest and possibly discuss with the Lord what the beheading of John the Baptist might mean. Disappointingly, the scene that greeted them was a carbon copy of what they

---

[1] All scriptural quotations, unless otherwise noted, are from the New American Standard Bible.

[2] Matthew 14:22-27; Mark 6:45-52; John 6:16-21

were trying to escape. Though frustrated with the absence of re-lief, the Master's response to the crowd awaiting them on the shore came as no surprise. He was who He was, and He did what He was here to do. His desire to lead the disciples to a lonely place for their benefit was replaced with a desire to reach out in teaching, ministry, and provision for the benefit of the 5,000 men plus women and children.

Now, free from the press of the crowd, the disciples joined in a unified effort, rhythmically propelling their vessel across the surface of the sea. The work of ministry had been exchanged for the labor required to traverse a rather unpredictable body of wa-ter. For a number of the crew, however, this was familiar territo-ry. Lives of netting fish had been interrupted by the call of the Nazarene to become fishers of men. They had replaced confident, cultivated careers with the innocence associated with their in-ternships. Everyday had been a new lesson, a new experience, or a new adventure. The demands, the disciplines, and the dynamics of following the Savior were not only thrilling, but also exhaust-ing. Now, disappointed that their respite had been denied, yet relieved that the responsibilities of ministry were behind them, the favored 12 were engaged in the escape that had been provid-ed. The former fishers of fish now led the rest in becoming sail-ors of the sea.

As darkness engulfed their world, a storm suddenly arose creating more than a formidable foe. Buffeted by wind and threatened by continuously heightening waves, the disciples ex-perienced the stark reality that human ingenuity and strength were not sufficient to battle the sheer forces of nature. Mark's description portrays them as *"straining at the oars"* (Mark 6:48).

The conversation experienced in that setting is not included in the divinely inspired accounts provided by the Gospel writers. Supposition and imagination can only conjure possible scenarios. Were the fiery personalities of James and John displayed? Did the over-confident, gregarious nature of Peter refuse to be abated? What about the others disciples—could it be the personalities and fears of each of the chosen suddenly took center stage? Did tempers flare? Were words exchanged? Noting that Jesus had sent them back across Galilee, is it possible that they questioned the wisdom of the Master? Humanity tends to reveal its base nature under stress and threat. The fact that these men had walked with Jesus on a daily basis, heard His teaching, viewed His compassion, and watched firsthand as He administered the miraculous did not change the reality of their circumstances, nor did it guarantee the automatic transformations of their dispositions. They were trapped in the authenticity of the moment and forced to deal with the real life pressures and uncertainties that surrounded them. The fact that they had been called, challenged, and commissioned did not alter the facts: the storm, their fatigue, their fear. They were struggling to survive and stretched beyond normal capacities to maintain their existence, let alone their direction.

While some were undoubtedly totally devoted to their survival, others may have been rather dubious about the value of the continuance of their efforts, feeling a sense of futility in the process. Whatever the original scene represented, the degree of their desperation became apparent as the scenario unfolds. Through the darkness, unfettered by the wind and storm, Jesus made His way toward them. The tumultuous sea simply provided a surface upon which the Savior would walk. The supernatural trumps the natural every time. As His figure came into view, His identity remained a mystery. The disciples who knew Him so well, had left their life occupations, and sacrificed personal dreams and ambitions to follow Him day after day, simply did not recognize him. They thought He was a ghost, an aberration of some kind. Not until Jesus spoke and identified himself did the disciples know it was the Lord. In the pressure of the moment— fighting fear and wrestling to survive—the chosen were merely men—susceptible to the realities of their environment.

It is important to pause at this juncture and realize that Jesus did not rebuke them for their weariness, confusion, frustration, fear, or lack of recognition. He simply reassured them of His presence, dissolved their fears, and restored their sense of security. Ah, the presence of the Lord and the appreciation of the same. Still today, His presence changes everything. However, there are times in our lives when His presence remains far from evident, when the storms of life blur any image we may have had of Him, when the struggle to survive looms so overwhelmingly we can only focus on the necessities presented by the threat we feel. We, too, like the twelve, can find ourselves "straining at the oars."

The focus becomes rather simple: what can we learn from this extraction of the Gospel account? What lessons might be afforded? What critical ideas are conveyed? A number of subjects will be addressed, though admittedly, not everything implied by the account will be examined in an attempt to find application for contemporary lives. However, critical matters faced by the disciples during this particular piece of their discipleship become targeted areas, drawing not only attention, but also insight, counsel, and instruction, enabling the reader to gain encouragement and motivation to be strong to the finish.

CHAPTER 2

Dealing with Disappointment

At the risk of adding details not given in the scriptural accounts, I would suggest that the disciples may well have been
disappointed when they arrived at Bethsaida.[3] The objective—
presumptuously within their minds—was to get away, take a
break, experience a respite; we might call it a holiday. When they
arrived, the size of the crowd that greeted them was not a welcomed sight. They had rowed across the lake anticipating some
time off, but that expectation evaporated into thin air once the
Master set His foot on dry ground. Matthew states, ***"And when
Jesus went ashore, He saw a great multitude, and felt compassion for them, and healed their sick."*** (Matthew 14:14). The
love Jesus felt upon their arrival may not have been what the disciples experienced as they faced the same set of circumstances. I
don't doubt their commitment or their ability to care, but I would
suggest that their humanity may well have overpowered their
spirituality at that moment. However, the Gospel writers do not
describe any reaction on the disciples' part. The only indicator is
their desire to send the multitude away, following a day of ministry. Regardless, it would seem only natural for disappointment to
set in.

Disappointment comes in all shapes and sizes. Furthermore,
it is not limited to any particular group of people. We all seem to
be granted the opportunity to share in this feature of a fallen
world. Basically, I think it safe to say, disappointment results
when expectations are not met. Sometimes that represents a
momentary feeling, a mere speed bump, while at other times the
disappointment presents a major hurdle that stands in the path,
challenging one's ability to proceed. The disappointment of not

---

[3] See Luke 9:10, 11.

having your favorite ice cream in the freezer holds no comparison to the feeling experienced when your date cancels at the last minute, your father fails to show up for your game, or the promotion you felt confident you would receive is granted to a fellow worker. The disciples knew disappointment and Jesus experienced disappointment. In like manner, we are no exception. We are all partakers in the common problem of disappointment. One need not live very long before learning the reality of this human norm.

The writer of Ecclesiastes[4] expresses his own feelings, showing a near displeasure with anything and everything, which he describes as *"striving after wind"* (Ecclesiastes 1:17). The futility of life resounds throughout the volume, declaring all to be vanity. To say the author had become disappointed with life might well be an understatement.

Sometimes disappointment can result in rather unusual circumstances. The story of Jonah comes to mind. God had called the prophet to warn the city of Nineveh of impending doom unless they repented. Nineveh, the capital of the ancient Assyrian Empire, eventually mustered the power to defeat and destroy the northern kingdom of Israel. Obviously, the task of preaching repentance to a wicked people was not one coveted by every prophet. Jonah resisted the call and had to be convinced that God was serious about His decision. However, it took being thrown overboard and being bathed in the stomach enzymes of a large fish to bring him to a place of surrender to the commission. As Jonah walked the streets of the city, one can only imagine the emotions he must have experienced. Nevertheless, the divine purpose was realized. In fact, once the message was preached, the city turned to God in mass.

Jonah was frustrated at their repentance. Why didn't God do what He said He was going to do and destroy this wicked, ungodly threat to the world? Jonah had warned them and he wanted to let the Almighty's wrath roll. Instead, God responded to the contrite cry of the people of Nineveh and offered forgiveness and grace, in keeping with His nature! Jonah, on the other hand,

---

[4] Qoheleth, the Preacher, who I believe to have been King Solomon.

wanted the hammer to fall and was disappointed at the show of God's compassion. Oh, my, how the recipients of grace can become irritated when grace is offered to someone else—especially when the recipient seems unworthy.

Solomon states, *"Hope deferred makes the heart sick"* (Proverbs 13:12). This creates a vivid picture of how disappointment can affect an individual. Expectations create a level of hope regarding the future, one's relationships, and/or the outcome of personal investments. When what was expected fails to materialize and hope dissipates, an internal emptiness results. At times, deep despondency can occur.

I don't know that it is possible to live in this world and be untouched by disappointment. The conditions in which we dwell fall far short of the garden designed and delivered by God for His prime creation to enjoy. Sin not only expelled Adam and Eve from their pristine home, but it also exposed them to a hostile environment. Not only would they face threats, danger, temptations, discord, and murder, but also disappointment. Simply said, some things don't change.

A review of experiences falling into this category could be depressing, but a simple illustration begs airing. During my junior year of high school, I was dating a young lady named Gayle. It was prom night and I was dressed in a suit and looking incredibly suave, waiting for Jim and Kathy to pick me up. We would then pick up Gayle and head for the big event. Jim and Kathy were both members of my class, had dated for some time, and would marry after graduation. I was dependent on friends at the time, since I did not own a car until my senior year. Furthermore, I really didn't want to use my dad's 1950 Studebaker. Jim came to the door, but as I prepared to go, my father voiced his objection. Up to this point, I had not discussed any details regarding the event. My dad expressed displeasure regarding a few things I had done recently, and now he disapproved my plan of going to a dance with a girl who was not up to his standards. He refused to give me permission to attend the dance. You must understand. I was raised in a very conservative Christian home. "We don't smoke, drink, dance or chew, or go with girls that do." I knew my father's position on the subject, but truly believed he would make an exception.

11

At this point and time in my life, one might think I could simply walk out and ignore my dad's objection, but I surely did not view this as an option. I tried to explain to my friends what had happened and why I couldn't go to the dance. Gayle, who had purchased a dress for the occasion, was waiting at her home, so I called her to let her know of the change of plans. Beings her home was just a couple blocks away, I walked to her house to spend the rest of the evening—doing what, I do not recall. What I do recall is disappointment.

Though hindsight may offer the opinion that it was not that big a deal, at the moment, it was huge. I was embarrassed, frustrated, angry, and incredibly disappointed. I felt disappointed in my father and horribly displeased in my inability to meet expectations, feeling like an absolute failure. Furthermore, I had let Gayle down. Surely, her parents would have questions for which I would have no reasonable answers, at least from my vantage point. To borrow from Solomon, my heart was sick.

Admittedly, I can recall other disappointments throughout my lifetime. I have known disappointments in relationships, in ventures attempted, and in the pursuit of goals and dreams. I experienced heartache through the failure to realize what had been planned; in expectations that produced a lot of promise, but never delivered. I am quite confident that I have not been alone in any of these arenas of life.

So, how should one deal with disappointment? Some might suggest the words of Alexander Pope hold the key. The famous eighteenth century English poet wrote: "Blessed is he who expects nothing, for he shall never be disappointed."[5] That may hold validity, but it surely offers no practicality. Three suggestions provide a more realistic process of dealing with this common occurrence.

First, deal with disappointment by considering the possibility of factors not immediately apparent. This holds true especially when dealing with other people: they didn't show up when you had planned, they didn't provide what you had expected, they

---

[5] Alexander Pope, "Disappointment Quotes," accessed March 17, 2017, http://www.goodreads.com/quotes/tag/disappointment.

didn't respond the way you had desired. Before jumping to conclusions, consider what else was involved, what else was taking place, or who else could be adversely affected. One would also be wise to consider the assumptions that might have kept the person from fulfilling your expectations.

Second, deal with disappointment by considering the possibility that your expectations were unreasonable or wrong. *Forbes* magazine featured an article that presented a list of eight expectations that will disappoint. I have added a question for each assumption as well as perspective personally gained regarding the expectation.

1. Life should be fair.

Question: What about life has given you any evidence to support this assumption? Though humans want to believe this is true, simple life experience proves it otherwise.

2. Opportunities will fall into my lap.

Question: Of the positions, opportunities, and privileges you currently enjoy, how many of them made their way into your life without your effort and commitment? Even if you were born into a rich family, life inevitably seems to reveal the reward goes to the diligent.

3. Everyone should like me.

Question: Are there people you don't like? If that is true, you realize others have made decisions about you, unfounded or otherwise. Sowing and reaping is a reality.

4. People should agree with me.

Question: Are you really that much brighter than everyone else? Even if you know you are right, people have their own opinions and wisdom demands respect for their perspective.

5. People know what I'm trying to say.

Question: Have you ever wondered if you knew what you were talking about? Proverbs 10:13 reads: ***"Through presumption comes nothing but strife."***

6. I'm going to fail.

Question: Do you not realize that accident favors a prepared mind? Your expectations usually precede your realizations. You need to believe it to receive it.

7. Things will make me happy.

Question: How many things that you now possess make you happy? For a season, you may find pleasure in things, but the contended life you desire will not merely come from more stuff.

8. I can change him/her.[6]

Question: How many people have you changed up to this point in your life? The only person you can change is yourself.

Third, deal with disappointment by considering what God may have in mind. One of the first things we need to consider when things are not going the way we expected has to do with this factor. What does God want to do? God always has a plan. Whether we are aware of His plan or not, we may find that we are mere participants in a much bigger scheme. We need to surrender to Him and trust His judgment, allowing ourselves to be players on the divine stage. In turn, we have the privilege of being a part of something exceptional. Resistance to God's plan, due to lack of understanding, yields the potential of ending up like Jonah.

Disappointment will come—it's a matter of when, not if. The fulfillment of our expectations has much to do with the level of satisfaction we realize. When life is less than gratifying, frustration and even outright anger may boil to the surface. Obviously, this not only affects the ability to handle the situation respectfully and responsibly, but it also reveals more about us than we

---

[6] Travis Bradberry, "Eight Unrealistic Expectations that Will Ruin You," accessed March 17, 2017, https://www.forbes.com/sites/travisbradberry/2016/08/02/8-unrealistic-expectations-that-will-ruin-you/#54f95f5819f0.

would probably choose to exhibit within the moment. Ah, yes! There's nothing like a dose of the difficulties of life to reveal our true nature and character. Ouch! Yet, there is another side to this possibility, another facet of the experience to consider.

Eliza Tabor Stephenson provides a great analogy: "Disappointment to a noble soul is what cold water is to burning metal; it strengthens, tempers, intensifies, but never destroys it."[7] Not everyone fits the description, noble soul. The response one demonstrates in the face of disappointment may well be a prime indicator of the presence or lack of any sense of nobility. If anyone should be blue blood, it should be a child of the Most High God. For King's Kids, disappointment must not be allowed to create a wall that prohibits progress, a sea of despair that drowns the testimony, or a fire that destroys the true character of the individual, or questions the depth of commitment. Suffice it to say, following Christ does not eliminate the realities of life, nor does it guarantee an easy passage through the same. Jesus left a promise that most of us do not want to claim: *"I have told you these things, so that in me you may have peace. In this world you will have trouble. But take heart! I have overcome the world"* (John 16:33, NIV, underlining added). The King James renders Christ's words as follows: *"These things I have spoken unto you, that in me ye might have peace. In the world ye shall have tribulation: but be of good cheer; I have overcome the world"* (underlining added). Both translations yield a simple truth: the disciples of Christ will experience difficulty. It seems to come with the territory and serves as a reminder that we live in a fallen world and sin has infected our sphere of existence. Sin does not, by its nature, produce peace and facilitate harmony and smooth sailing. Consequently, living on planet earth will include the realization of the fruit of the seed sown back in the Garden of Eden, and which people continue to sow and reap. Trouble, which comes in many shapes and sizes, provides one expression of that fruit. This could be experienced through anything from

---

[7] Eliza Tabor Stephenson, "Quote by Eliza Tabor Stephenson," accessed September 8, 2017. https://www.goodreads.com/quotes/283812-disappointment-to-a-noble-soul-is-what-cold-water-is.

persecution to disappointment, and a multitude of options in-between. Admittedly, without intentional cultivation and in spite of prayers for crop failure, all of us experience the bitter taste of the realities of life from time to time.

Accepting the inability to escape this negative aspect of our existence, one must contemplate what affect the condition will be allowed to have. I truly believe that much of what will be experienced is predetermined. Let me explain. An individual who faces temptation or difficulty obviously has the ability to overcome or surrender, assuming the position of a victim. I propose that decision is usually not made within the moment, but rather over time. The right conclusion will be the outgrowth of disciplines embraced, habits altered, commitments made, and a lifestyle chosen. Undoubtedly, the unexpected can occur; brand new experiences may simply arise. Yet, the strength gained through "spiritual conditioning" renders the individual sufficient to the task. My mind runs to the fifth chapter of Romans where Paul writes: ***"And not only this*** [referring to the eternal hope we have gained in Christ]***, but we also exult in our tribulations, knowing that tribulation brings about perseverance; and perseverance, proven character; and proven character, hope; and hope does not disappoint"*** (Romans 5:3-5a, parenthetical statement added). Through the process of life, one experiences many things and each event holds the possibility to destroy or strengthen. With faith enacted, commitment engaged, and pure resolve applied, each negative experience yields a positive result. Lessons are learned as well as character molded. The outcome translates into a victory for the potential victim.

God knows in advance the potential each encounter holds. His Word promises the ability to overcome whatever difficulties or challenges we are allowed to face (c.f. 1 Corinthians 10:13). Simple understanding of the sovereignty of God provides assurance that His allowance serves a purpose. He will guard us against that which will overwhelm and destroy, just as a good parent does with his or her child. However, some experiences are allowed for the sake of growth and development. God safe guards us against other difficulties due to our inability to handle the challenge at the given point and time.

Though human parents are limited in their ability to protect their child from the overpowering experiences, God is not. Consequently, when disappointment—or any other negative occurrence—arrives, the question should not be *why*, but rather *what*: "What do you want me to learn, Lord?" "What might I gain or benefit from this experience?" Time will tell, and the next confrontation with difficulty—possibly disappointment—will undoubtedly reveal lessons learned and growth realized.

As surely as disappointment comes, so will the results of expanded understanding, strength, and trust in the Lord. Each encounter along life's journey holds the potential for negative or positive impact. The outcome, however, remains the decision of each disciple—to be overwhelmed and defeated or to overcome and be triumphant.

CHAPTER 3

Obedience Required of Disciples

Referencing Matthew's account of the story, we discover that Jesus *"made the disciples get into the boat and go before him to the other side"* (Matthew 14:22). The disciples did not practice an escape, an alternative, a flippant response, or some logical follow-up to the previous event. Their response was the direct result of the instruction of the Lord. Jesus sensed His need to be alone with the Father and He went to the mountain to pray. This leads to a lesson within the lesson. Strength and encouragement can often be found in praying with others, but there are times when simple one-on-one face time with God is essential and irreplaceable. Corporate prayer is powerful, no doubt. However, relationships demand intimacy, time alone with each other, sharing thoughts, concerns, and desires that are simply too personal or too critical for group interaction.

I love time with the family and truly enjoy the conversation, laughter, discussion, and camaraderie realized on such occasions. Such times produce not only meaningful moments, but often lasting memories. However, my marriage has not been built on such encounters and junctures. There was a time when it was just the two of us, the grassroots of our fifty plus years of marriage, our children, and grandchildren. On many occasions, we had talked about, prayed over, discussed, considered, and planned many things that had not been shared with the larger loop. Oh, no doubt, in time, pieces of those private conversations became common knowledge within our family circle, but propriety required personal communion first. Yet, it goes far beyond the conversations held or the information shared. This speaks to the basis of relationship—time, time alone. Time to share, time to grow, time to learn about each other, time to permit each other to become a little more vulnerable. Time to allow the oneness described in Scripture to become a reality in the marriage (cf.

Genesis 2:24; Matthew 19:5; Ephesians 5:31). Without the strength of that relationship—developed, enhanced, and reaffirmed within the realms of the private—would there be the possibility of valuable and meaningful family times? So it is in our relationship with God.

Going to church, fellowshipping with other believers, engaging in worship and receiving instruction and admonition from the presentation of God's Word are valuable experiences. Such encounters provide energy, strength, enjoyment, growth, and memories. However, for a true Christian relationship to grow, private, personal time is needed—personal time with God. Too often the emphasis can be on Christians being with other Christians. In so doing, one can ignore the true need and the most important factor. If Jesus, the Son of God, thought having time for personal communion with the Father was essential, how dare we, His fallen though redeemed creation, assume it to be anything less than critical? After all, without a real, ongoing, growing relationship with God, what is church? What is the fellowship of believers? Back to the subject at hand: obedience.

Obedience to God's voice has been understood as a critical mass from the beginning. Emphasized throughout the pages of God's Word, the necessity of obedience has received testimony from the lives and expressions of men and women desiring to live meaningful and purposeful lives. Today, preachers preach sermons, artists sing songs, and people engage in serendipitous conversations fostering an ongoing awareness of the principle. Yet challenge might be brought to the willingness of the average church goer to be a true God follower.

The failure to obey God afforded Adam and Eve the left foot of fellowship, introducing them to a strange environment outside the presence of God. The human family quickly learned the fallacy of disobedience. Noah, on the other hand, obeyed God, providing escape and provision for all who would believe, though only his family experienced the Ark. Abraham was called to obedience, the final proof of his compliance demonstrated within his response to a divine appointment on Mount Moriah (Genesis 22). The instruction to offer his son—his only son, his long-awaited son—resulted in an altar created uniquely for the moment. Undoubtedly this challenged all that Abraham believed about the

God who had called him and made incredible promises to him. Ultimately, the patriarch would come to know that God did not desire sacrifice but obedience.

The first king of Israel learned this lesson the hard way. His reign began with glowing promise, knowing God's anointing, provision, and direction. After experiencing victory over the Amalekites (1 Samuel 15), Saul thought he had a better idea than God's direction, so he allowed the Israelites to keep the spoil of battle and spared Agag, the king, even though God had given clear instructions: *"Strike Amalek and utterly destroy all that he has"* (1 Samuel 15:3). Samuel, the prophet, was sent to confront the monarch's disobedience and announce that God had rejected him as leader of His people. A piece of Samuel's pronouncement has become well-known and leaves a lesson for all willing learners: *"To obey is better than sacrifice, and to heed than the fat of rams"* (v. 22).

The disciples did not seem to question their responsibility to obey the Lord. Consequently, they entered the boat and started their trek across the Sea of Galilee. Maybe they were simply relieved, having no further responsibility, and thought that possibly the original plan was still intact. They were going to get away. Being sent across the sea was not an unexpected assignment, as they had traversed these waters many times. Facing a storm while in route was not unusual, as research indicates storms in the region commonly arose without warning. Whether as fishermen or as disciples, crossing the Sea of Galilee in less than peaceful conditions was always a possibility.

On one such crossing, Christ demonstrated His authority over the winds and the waves, boggling the minds of His followers. Awakened from his sleep, He spoke, *"Hush, be still"* (Mark 4:39). The tumultuous sea immediately became calm, the wind stopped, and peace replaced panic. On this particular voyage across the same body of water, Jesus was not with them. Without the Master in the boat, the threat of the moment began to take its toll— wind blowing, waves pounding, visibility decreasing, and strength waning. The disciples faced the possibility of not only losing their way, but losing their lives. Needless to say, their obedience had not led them to experience smooth sailing.

The idea of obedience has come under increased scrutiny, contributing to the modern mentality of resisting authority. In 1961, social psychologist, Stanley Milgram, conducted an experiment with the primary objective of studying human obedience to authority. The trial of Adolph Eichmann, famed Nazi exterminator, which had been televised, served as a backdrop to the scientific investigation. In Milgram's 1974 book, he published his findings and associated conclusions. He describes how a person surrenders his or her will to an authority, entering an "agentic state." For subordinates of Hitler in Germany and Stalin in Russia, this state was a "profound slumber" compared to the "light doze" of subjects in his lab, but the process was the same. Once a person merges with an authority that gives the orders and enters the twilight zone of the agentic state, even though the authority might be doing inhumane things that are "alien to his nature," the person under authority feels "virtually guiltless."[8]

Milgram proposed that individuals lending themselves subject to authority fall vulnerable to cults, etc. History lends credence to the supposition, from political regimes to religious movements. However, to throw the baby out with the bath water seems horribly immature and less than intellectually responsible. Australian psychologist, Gina Perry, refutes Milgram's theory in her published volume, citing Milgram's research and the inconsistencies within his own findings.[9] However, the research and supposition continues regarding obedience to authority.

Considered one of the greatest historians of the nineteenth century, Lord Acton's commonly quoted statements fuels the ongoing fire: "Power tends to corrupt and absolute power corrupts absolutely. Great men are almost always bad men, even when they exercise influence and not authority; still more when you superadd the tendency of the certainty of corruption by authori-

---

[8] "The Shocking Truth of the Notorious Milgram Obedience Experiments," Blog, accessed May 22, 2018, http://blogs.discovermagazine.com/crux/2013/10/02/the-shocking-truth-of-the-notorious-milgram-obedience-experiments/#.WLn9wBiZNmB.

[9] Gina Perry, *Behind the Shock Machine: The Untold Story of the Notorious Milgram Psychology Experiments* (New York, NY: The New Press, 2013).

ty."[10] Unfortunately, in most references, the word "tends" fails to be included, and the complete statement rarely appears. No doubt, people have inappropriately and destructively used positions of authority. However, the failure of those in authority to practice the stewardship of the privilege with prudence, understanding, and sensitivity does not invalidate the value and necessity of authority.

One must incorporate all factors in the equation before coming to a valid conclusion. For example, one must include two factors before any application of Acton's assumption be made toward the Creator. First, God is not a man; therefore, human frailty must never be associated with Him. God is impeccable, holy, and pure. Consequently, tendencies synonymous with His final creation simply do not apply. God called the disciples to obey Jesus Christ, the expression of God as man. Second, although Jesus was born as a frail human, this did not diminish Him to the point of possessing the sinful nature of man. You see, Jesus became one of us, but He did not become just like us. Otherwise, we would have no one to become like. The disciples did not receive directions from a guy with an opinion. They received instruction from God incarnate. Jesus was worthy of the disciples' obedience. No misuse of authority lay within reach; no tendency toward corruption existed.

Obedience as a human behavior implies two factors: (1) the recognition of an authority figure, and (2) the willingness of the person under authority to respond in a positive manner. The act of obedience reflects a sense of responsibility to do so or a motive that prompts the response. The authority figure might be a parent, teacher, coach, police officer, boss, supervisor, or person of higher rank—such as a military, religious, or governmental figure. The person in authority may have been granted authority by a recognized figure, such as the authority a parent gives to a babysitter.

The motivation behind a person's response may be much harder to gauge. Though a number of possible underlying rea-

---

[10] Lord Acton, "Lord Acton Quote Archive," Action Institute, accessed March 5, 2017, https://acton.org/research/lord-acton-quote-archive.

sons for obedience may exist, a few major incentives quickly come to mind. Fear may serve as motivation as the person simply obeys in order to avoid the reprisal or punishment associated with disobedience. Learned response must be included in any consideration of motivation. Hebrews 5:8 indicates that Jesus *"learned obedience from the things which He suffered."* Respect also serves as a motive in a person's response. This would most obviously be illustrated in the military. Parents would ostensibly like to believe this stands behind their child's favorable reaction to their instructions, though, at times, fear may serve as a more likely stimulus. Fear of arrest, fines, or imprisonment could motivate obedience to the law. However, some individuals choose to obey the law out of respect and a moral responsibility as a citizen of a society or country. Derived benefit also serves as motivation implying a reward follows compliance. However, love may be the strongest motive of all.

No doubt, a believer's response to God involves a combination of motives: fear, respect, derived benefit, and love. Scripture teaches believers to fear the Lord. All too often, this idea implies a negative view of God, the ultimate authority, who stands willing to crush anyone who even considers failure to respond. *Yare*, the Hebrew word most often used in the Old Testament to convey this concept, though associated with the idea of fear or dread, also speaks of reverence, awe, and honor. The full scope of meaning may well depend on the person's relationship with God. Defiance, rebellion, and/or disregard would suggest a literal fear of God, yielding a somewhat negative perspective. However, relationship with the Almighty, through faith in Jesus Christ, offers a different understanding. In this case, the fear of the Lord speaks of the desire to show limitless respect, deep love, and adoration. God calls us to this response.

As the Savior prepared to fulfill the Father's plan and assume the role for which He had appeared on the stage of life, He met with the chosen twelve and shared some heartfelt final instructions and admonitions. The setting was the Passover, the ancient feast to be celebrated before his appointment with the cross. The occasion, as described in John 13-16, reveals many of the priorities the Savior wanted His followers to remember and put into practice once He was gone. From that encounter, these words are lifted for our contemporary application: *"If you love Me, you will keep My commandments"* (John 14:15). True discipleship may well be interpreted as entering an "agentic state," as described by Milgram, meaning obedience to authority. In fact, a disobedient disciple would be an oxymoron. Discipleship requires obedience.

Watchman Nee, in his highly acclaimed classic, *Spiritual Authority*, lends critical understanding: "Now because both authority and obedience have been instituted by God, it is natural for those who know God and Christ to obey. ... He who accepts Christ accepts the principle of obedience. Hence a person who is filled with Christ must be one who is also filled with obedience."[11]

I see love, trust, and obedience as closely connected when it comes to this area of life. If I love someone, I learn to trust them. In doing so, I am more likely to obey them when they ask me to do certain things, especially when obedience requires getting out of my comfort zone. When I obey and find it beneficial, my level of trust increases and my degree of love and respect is enhanced. As the love grows, the trust grows, and vice versa. Consequently, obedience becomes easier and easier. Jesus' words confirm this suggestion. If I say I love Him but do not obey Him, I confess my lack of trust in Him and reveal an immature love, at best. This formula was at the heart of our Lord's confrontation and conversation with Peter after the resurrection. Possibly you will remember the story, as described in John 21.

The disciples had gone fishing—a suggestion announced by Peter and adopted by the rest. The venture was undoubtedly out of frustration and confusion more than a desire for recreation. Jesus had been crucified but reappeared three days later—alive and well. However, the elation they felt with His resurrection was counterbalanced with the news that He had completed His work and would be leaving them—going back to heaven and His Father. As the disciples spread their nets and followed learned routines, they realized absolutely nothing for their trouble. Jesus stood on the bank the following morning and spoke these words: *"Children, you do not have any fish, do you"* (John 21:5)? That's

---

[11] Watchman Nee, *Spiritual Authority* (New York, NY: Christian Fellowship Publishers, 1972), 47.

enough to make the blood boil. "Children." Did He really call them that? Yet, the disciples followed His instruction to cast their nets on the opposite side of the boat and were shocked and amazed at the bounty of their catch, barely able to pull it into the boat.

Peter put on his "outer garment" (not a normal thing to do when going swimming) and made his way to shore. He had to see Jesus up close and personal. There, after eating the breakfast Jesus had fixed for them, Jesus confronted Peter three times with a simple question: Do you love Me more than these? Though one could discuss the theological and psychological implications and inferences afforded in this passage, I would suggest that Jesus was addressing the triangular relationship to which the disciple had been called: love, trust, and obedience. It would prove to be critical in Peter's life, as it is in ours as well. Needless to say, if one professes to be a Christian, a disciple of Christ, and fails to obey God and His Word, the legitimacy of confession might be questioned based on the love and obedience demonstrated in the relationship. The words of our Lord quickly come back to mind: "Do you love me more than these?"

CHAPTER 4

Obedience Does Not Guarantee Smooth Sailing

Naivety may be delightful in children, but it can be devastating for those beyond the age of innocence. For example, too many people hold the opinion that if they do the right thing, everything will go right. History, experience, and the Word of God yield a different conclusion, and this reality can seriously challenge one's confidence and faith. We observe this factor at play in the story before us.

The followers of Christ had just endured a long day and failed to realize the reason they had journeyed to this particular area. The previous story reveals that Jesus had suggested they take a break. The news of Herod's beheading of John the Baptist created the need for a respite. Not only impacted by the account, the Scripture reveals the hectic-ness of their schedule. Mark reports: *"For there were many people coming and going, and they did not even have time to eat"* (Mark 6:31b). Consequently, Jesus said, *"Come away by yourselves to a lonely place and rest a while"* (31a). They had anticipated a much needed period of respite. The disciples did not realize the intent of their journey, however, but an eager crowd anticipated the itinerary and awaited them on the other shore when their boat moored. Instead of relaxation, they were thrust into ministry, assisting the Lord in His commitment to meet the people's needs.

As the sun began to set and the day drew to a close, the disciples begged Jesus to send the crowd away; they needed something to eat. The Lord's simple response created the backdrop for the only miracle recorded in all four gospels—the feeding of the five thousand: *"They do not need to go away; you give them something to eat!"* (Matthew 14:16). With the people fed, both spiritually and physically, Jesus sent the disciples on ahead so He could spend time alone with the Father once everyone was gone. In the course of following Christ's directive, they found themselves facing a hostile wind and growing weary in the struggle. How could this be? Had they not followed the Lord's instruction, proceeding in total obedience? Is one not guaranteed smooth sailing if he or she does what the Lord instructs?

The Book of Proverbs has long provided a great source of inspiration and guidance. While the words of this old, sacred collection should not be received as promises or commandments, the principles afford tremendous insight. These learned truths yielded from the daily experiences of life have been passed on from generation to generation. One such axiom has proven to be personally helpful: ***"Through presumption comes nothing but strife, but with those who receive counsel is wisdom"*** (Proverbs 13:10). Practical application finds not only a place in the natural world, but the spiritual world as well. Presumption regarding God's will yielding perfect peace, ease of progress, and even instant success has truly brought frustration, misunderstanding, and possibly even loss of faith. The right path does not ensure an easy path!

Moses learned the lesson firsthand. The elation spawned by deliverance from slavery in Egypt was soon replaced by the harsh realities of life in the wilderness. God had promised the Israelites a land flowing with milk and honey. It was a land given to Abraham, father of the nation, and destined for his offspring. Following the guidance God afforded them via a pillar of cloud by day and a pillar of fire by night, the former slaves experienced God's provision and protection. However, they also endured difficulty, disappointment, disillusionment, and desperation. Moses also experienced challenges. Though he followed God's instructions at the burning bush and multiple subsequent divine encounters, he suffered the criticism and rebellion of the people he tried to assist. The wind in his face remained steady for 40 years. And if that wasn't enough, his obedience was not rewarded as he might have expected.

The Old Testament prophets delivered the word of the Lord in difficult times to less than receptive audiences. One prophet, in particular, suffered for his submission to the Almighty's instruction. Jeremiah was a prophet to Judah during the years leading up to the Babylonian defeat of Jerusalem. His ministry continued to the exiled Jews, encouraging them to believe God's promise of restoration and renewal. For his trouble, Jeremiah knew isolation, imprisonment, physical abuse, and attempts on his life, all in the process of his obedience.

The Apostle Paul's life truly illustrated this reality. From the moment of his heavenly encounter on the road to Damascus (Acts 9), continual confrontation, persecution, difficulty, and distress complicated his life and resisted his ministry, all in response to his obedience. Even his voyage to Rome to face Caesar and lend testimony to his faith and the gospel message—ordained by the Lord—was less than smooth sailing (Acts 27-28).

Other followers of Christ have known less than immediate reward for their diligent response to the direction of the Lord. James, the brother of John, was beheaded by Herod. Stephen, one of the first deacons in the Christian church of Jerusalem, was stoned for his efforts to preach the gospel. Peter experienced imprisonment; John was exiled to the Isle of Patmos; early Christians were fed to lions, and every day, in the twenty-first century, true believers are subjected to persecution, incarceration, and even death.

No greater example of this reality can be projected than the Savior, Jesus Christ the Lord. Jesus came into our world, born of a woman; He experienced life in the vulnerability of a human body as opposed to a divine being. This was the Father's plan. However, being obedient to the plan did not afford Jesus effortless days, uncomplicated relationships, or automatic achievements. His road was hard; His life demanding. Everything He experienced was leading up to rejection, deception, prosecution, and death. Yet, this was the will of God. Christ did not stumble on His journey and fall into trouble due to disobedience. His perfect submission led to His crucifixion.

When speaking of the crucifixion of Jesus, most people understand the reason for the suffering that resulted from Christ's obedience. It was the Father's plan; it was required as the penalty for sin. Jesus understood the plan. His words to the disciples[12]

---

[12] "Saying 'The Son of Man must suffer many things, and be rejected by the elders and chief priests and scribes, and be killed, and be raised up on the third

lend evidence to this claim. Jesus' prayer in the Garden of Gethsemane reiterates His understanding of what stood before Him. The writer of Hebrews records that Jesus *"learned obedience from the things which He suffered"* (Hebrews 5:8). Did this mean that Jesus had a proclivity toward disobedience? Again, I reference the fact that Jesus became a man, but did not assume the fallen nature of humanity. As a man, He required lessons in obedience. It was as preparation for him to serve as a high priest who could *"sympathize with our weaknesses"* and be *"tempted in all things as we are"* (Hebrews 4:15). By doing the will of the Father, in spite of what His submission cost Him, Jesus experienced the reality of obedience—what it feels like, what it means. Needless to say, the cost involved in obedience provided great benefit. This may not serve as a satisfactory example because we find it hard to compare ourselves with Jesus. I will add, however, that I believe obedience to God's authority always yields benefit.

The experience of Moses and the Israelites might serve as an example to which we can more readily relate. They followed God's direction, but did not find the journey easy, convenient, or free from complication. The travel was difficult: terrain, climate, a mass of humanity trying to travel together across an uncharted wilderness, and enemies that would attempt to obstruct their progress. So, why did so many problems accompany obedience? Let's consider a few possibilities.

First, the Israelites needed to learn to trust God. It may be said that trust is not learned until it is required. The people may have presumed that God would do whatever they needed Him to do. However, they learned a simple yet difficult lesson: most often God does what is really needed in the face of trials and possibilities, even though the recipients of His intervention may not understand. As slaves, the Israelites had relied on their own wits, while occasionally benefitting from the grace and provisions of their owners. As abhorrent as slavery may have been, they might have developed a sense of self-sufficiency. In the dessert, they

---

day'" (Luke 9:22). Also, see v. 44; Matthew 16:21, 17:22, 23. The Old Testament holds numerous references to the suffering and death of the Messiah, primarily in the Psalms and the prophets. The most well-known is Isaiah 53.

were totally vulnerable and came to know a fear that, at times, became paralyzing. God wanted them to trust Him. The difficulties incorporated in their journey left few other options.

Second, God wanted to grow His people, enabling them to face the difficulties that lie ahead. This suggested reality leads to a simple principle: God is more interested in our character than our comfort. As one reads the Exodus story, the complaining and grumbling of the former slaves becomes a dominant theme. They longed for the food of Egypt and the familiarities of their previous existence. Though slaves, they had predictable lives. The wilderness journey thrust them into a world of unknowns. Furthermore, they were forced to trust their future into the hands of one who may have appeared as the possessor of questionable credentials. He had been the adopted grandson of Pharaoh. Then he made a run-for-his-life due to a presumption regarding his place in the scheme of things, which led to the murder of an Egyptian. For the next forty years, Moses had lived as a lowly shepherd working for his father-in-law. Through his testimony of a face-to-face encounter with God and the demonstration of miraculous signs, the Israelites chose him as their deliverer. Undoubtedly, the difficulties of the journey and the many unknowns caused the people to lack confidence in Moses' leadership abilities.

God's primary concern, however, was not focused on what they ate, drank, how they felt, or if they liked everything that was happening at any given moment. Oh, He had not lost any love for Israel. He simply could not ignore the immaturity, self-centeredness, and lack of character they exhibited. Their tomorrows would require more than what had been necessary yesterday. Consequently, this time of preparation was a critical piece. As illogical as it may have seemed in the moment, this was, without doubt, an expression of God's love.

Third, the enemy seldom, if ever, allows God's children to proceed unhindered. Satanic interference can often be overplayed, assigning everything that happens to the enemy's doing. I refuse to even consider him as omnipotent. However, Satan will attack the children of God at any time, on any level, with no regret, and no consideration. A very simple but thoroughly thought-through bit of theology offers explanation as to why.

I offer a simple principle to help lend understanding. If someone has an enemy against whom they seek revenge, but the enemy is stronger, more powerful, and more capable than the one seeking retribution, what can be done? A direct attack on the enemy would be useless, or so it would seem. A rather simple approach would be to attack the enemy's family or children.

From what we deduce from Scripture, Satan, an archangel named Lucifer, was once a submissive, trusted agent of the Most High. However, Lucifer decided to take matters into his own hands; he would make himself like God (Isaiah 14:12-20; Ezekiel 28:14-19). His decision led to his expulsion from the Kingdom and he became the enemy of God. Totally aware of God's power, Satan recognized the impossibility of direct revenge so he often settles for the next best thing—to attack His children. Israel was the target, and revenge was the motive.

Through it all, the faithfulness of the Lord was continually experienced. In fact, the opposition of the enemy only proved advantageous in solidifying Moses' leadership and reaffirming God's demonstrations of power and provision. Consequently, even the enemy's best efforts, in time, only revealed the benefits of obedience. No, the children of Israel were not perfect in their obedience. Moses, though stellar throughout much of the process, had his moments of failure as well. Despite their flaws, they continued to move in the right direction and, ultimately, reached their destination—the Promise Land. The journey was neither smooth nor easy. Nevertheless, the people of Israel realized the goal, learned much needed lessons, and established God's purposes.

Some of my favorite people are those who have spent their lives in service to others. More times than not, such devotion comes as a result of God's calling and design for one's life. Over my years in ministry, I have encountered a number of such exceptional individuals. Jim and Patsy Macauley come to mind. In writing this chapter, it seemed only prudent and appropriate to interview these two giants of the faith to illustrate the need for obedience, despite the complications that may accompany that obedience.

During my interview with the Macauleys, Jim shared their story. They arrived in Nigeria in 1968 with a sense of hope, excitement, and assurance that this was God's direction for their lives. Upon arrival, Jim, Patsy, and their three children faced immediate difficulties. They needed to learn to drive on the left side of the road as well as gain the use of a new, but difficult language. In addition to these small adjustments, they were introduced to a country embroiled in a civil war that would continue for the next two years. They faced constant road checks and often had guns pointed at them. As they faced continual scrutiny, they learned simple gestures to show their compliance and cooperation. One such habit was to turn on the dome light immediately after being stopped to allow the soldiers to confirm identity. As his face broke into a smile, Jim noted that the people couldn't seem to hear the difference between the words "mercenary" and "missionary." The greatest difficulty was getting a handle on the new culture—a culture defined by many unique characteristics.

Forty Assemblies of God missionaries resided in Nigeria at the time the Macauleys arrived. Soon they discovered that they would help lead a transition in the mission strategy for the country that would move the Nigerian church to a more indigenous position by training pastors to lead with confidence and effectiveness, and giving support and encouragement to the national church. This attrition took place as retiring missionaries could not be replaced and missionaries who had reached the end of their visas found the government unwilling to issue a renewal. This meant a major reduction in the number of U.S. missionaries in the country. The Bible school was a key component. At the start, the school had approximately 50-75 students. Immediately it became apparent that new bylaws were needed as well as the issuance of a printing press. By the time the Macauleys transferred to Ethiopia, the school was running 630 students with 24 fully degreed faculty members. Today the school boasts 1,200 students with a second school developed later, which runs 1,000 students.

Over their 25 year investment, the Macauleys would bury two fellow missionaries, live under constant threats and challenges, and Jim would battle malaria more than thirty times. In fact, their physician in the United Stated facilitated their move to a different country due to concerns that Jim might not survive another encounter with the disease. As a result, the Assemblies of God

World Missions, the Fellowship with which they served, redirected their efforts, assigning them to serve in Ethiopia.

The Macauleys arrived in Ethiopia with two suitcases in hand. No Assemblies of God church had been established and they did not have relationships with any national pastors, fellowships, or organizations. In essence, they were starting from scratch. Jim described their early efforts as "in the process." Unafraid and confident in the Lord, they faced the future with optimism. How? Why? Twenty-five years of experience in Nigeria had taught them that when God directs, He provides.

The years that followed yielded a recognized, registered church, an established Bible school, a strong relationship with the national church, trained pastors who functioned in solid leadership roles and great harmony in the Christian community. When Patsy had a heart attack, the couple returned to the United States earlier than planned. I asked if they had any regrets. Jim rather shyly responded that they wish they could have served a couple more years. I smiled and said, "If I know you, Jim, it never would have been enough. You would have died in Africa." He laughed, nodded his head and said, "You're right."

One theme that repeatedly surfaced was the fact that their previous experiences had prepared them for the current difficulties. Though, at times, it literally seemed hopeless, previous experiences had conditioned them to handle tough times. Spiritual opposition, cultural resistance, governmental hindrances, and the endless demands of people-in-need created constant complications and barriers, yet they never felt defeated. They knew they had been obedient. In spite of obstacles, difficulties, and delays, they recognized their dependence on God and did not waver in their faith.

Obedience does not guarantee smooth sailing. In the midst of rough times, one should keep in mind a couple factors. First, God is a faithful father who does not play games with His children. Everything He allows has a reason and will ultimately prove beneficial. In the moment of crisis, one may question God's purposes, but the development of His children necessitates a process that facilitates growth and maturity as well as a simple reliance on God that goes beyond complete comprehension. Easy, convenient circumstances do not promote an increase in character, strength, endurance, or trust. The Father wants His children to progress in perspective and capability. The option of allowing them to remain as children—pampered and totally protected— does not accomplish His desires or realize His purposes. God is patient, but He is also persistent.

Second, we must realize that we only see a very small portion of what God sees. What we envision falls far short of the divine plan. This subject will be addressed more fully in chapter eleven. Suffice it to say, obeying God's Word and trusting in His capabilities, as opposed to our own, may not always seem attractive at the moment. However, because God knows what He is doing, why would we not want to join Him in the adventure?

CHAPTER 5

Fear Vexes Even the Faithful

In reading Scripture, one soon becomes aware of how often the words "do not be afraid" or "fear not" appear. Fear falls into the category of a very common human experience. Literature is replete with famous quotes and favorite stories that thrill the hearer with tales of overcoming the menace. However, few people, if any, have ever lived without confronting fear. Truth be told, fear can be beneficial. The fear of a deadly snake, the fear of an oncoming train, or the fear of mishandling a loaded firearm may well prolong one's life. Fear based upon the knowledge of certain outcomes leads to good decisions and appropriate actions. To deny the negative possibilities and proceed without caution may sound appealing to movie goers, but this approach seldom proves prudent for people living in the real world.

On the other hand, fear must not be a controlling factor. For instance, many accomplishments, discoveries, victories, and revelations would never have become reality if people allowed fear to dominant. Life continually affords opportunities, veiled in unknowns that create anxiety, reservation, and alarm. Consequently, too many people walk away, shrink back, and refuse the invitation to conquer the fear and know the thrill of moving beyond previous limits and gaining new ground. Eleanor Roosevelt stated, "You gain strength, courage, and confidence by each experience in which you really stop to look fear in the face. You are able to say to yourself, 'I have lived through this horror. I can take the next thing that comes along.' You must do the thing you think you cannot do."[13]

---

[13] Eleanor Roosevelt, "Fear," Proverbia.net, accessed March 11, 2017, http://en.proverbia.net/citastema.asp?tematica=464.

Undoubtedly the disciples knew the reality of fear as they faced the elements, encased in the darkness of a stormy night. Matthew 14:24 indicates they were *"battered by the waves; for the wind was contrary."* Although a number of the disciples had been fishermen before becoming followers of Jesus, their experiences may have heightened their concerns over an angry sea and a strong wind, rather than diminishing them. As the hours passed and the struggle continued, doubt may have replaced confidence. John's Gospel states that they had rowed three or four miles (6:19). Having rowed a boat in normal conditions, I can only imagine the toll created by wrestling the wind and waves for that length of time. As fatigue contributed to the mix, the mighty became weak.

Some might challenge the assumption of fear being present in this scenario, but the disciples' reaction to the sight of the Savior walking on the water would seem to affirm their fear. Mark 6:50-51 reads: *"But when they saw Him walking on the sea, they supposed that it was a ghost, and cried out; for they all saw Him and were frightened."* Now, it is well to remember that at this point they had walked with the Lord for quite some time, knew His voice, and were able to recognize His form quite easily. However, their view was blurred by the storm and their perception was skewed by the presence of fear.

Some people might suggest that true believers and faithful followers of Christ should never experience fear. Nice theory, but becoming a Christian does not eliminate our humanity. Though the Spirit dwells within, we remain in the flesh. God knows our frame (Psalm 103:14); He knows our weaknesses and the Spirit prays for us (Romans 8:25-27). He knows our tendency to be fearful, but there is no condemnation (Romans 8:1). We should give a shout of praise when we realize that God is not as hard on us as our fellow Christians or as we are on ourselves. Remember how often Scripture encourages us to "Fear not!" As long as we dwell in the flesh we will experience the insecurities and anxieties that accompany life in the natural realm. Undoubtedly we will overcome our fears as we mature and learn to trust the Father beyond our understanding. We must always remember: He is never afraid and He always knows the ultimate outcome. The only unknown is how we will respond.

The disciples did not display perfection. In fact, their humanity often became evident. They had lived with the Creator of the universe, 24-7 for the space of three years. They knew something special was taking place as they heard His words, witnessed Him performing miracles, and sensed the divine ordination of His presence and purpose. They knew someone special had come into their world. They experienced moments of revelation, yet questions remained. Peter even boldly declared Christ's divine identity (Matthew 16:16), yet questioned whether He was the promised Messiah whom the prophets had foretold. Even though his heart said, "Yes," his mind still experienced doubt. The space between the heart and the mind can leave room for fear, especially when things seem less than predictable.

The cloak of darkness over the Sea of Galilee, complicated by the robust wind and growing swells, took the disciples out of their comfort zone and thrust them into consternation. As conditions worsened, their fear and concern grew. Although the Gospel accounts do not record their conversation, one can only imagine what they said in the midst of this storm in the middle of the night. Quite possibly they verbalized their fears and expressed intense panic.

When I was about seven years old, my mother, sister, and I went to visit my Uncle Archer in Oakland, California. Late one night, my Mom and I stayed up to watch a movie on television. Mind you, we did not have a TV in our home so I was mesmerized by the magic of the box. We were watching a black and white horror movie. The only part of the movie that I recall was a large portrait hanging over the fireplace in a large living room. At night, eyes would appear in the portrait, looking for victims. Later during the night, someone would disappear.

While enduring the movie, I slipped away to use the restroom. In the darkness of the stairwell leading to the bathroom, my imagination ran wild. Then, as I made my way out of the bathroom onto the dimly lit balcony overlooking the living room, my Mother, who had hidden at the top of the steps, hollered, "Boo!" My shock brought an involuntary response; I punched her as hard as I could. Fortunately, as a skinny little kid, I didn't have must strength, so she did not sustain an injury. I couldn't believe I hit my Mom! Nevertheless, my life experience taught me that fear can induce thought processes and actions that might otherwise be unthinkable.

Fear is a powerful emotion. It can paralyze movement, blur vision, distort truth, and initiate physical reactions such as dilation of the pupils, increase of the heart rate, elevation of blood pressure, or spike one's blood sugar levels. Body systems not needed at the moment, such as the digestive system or immune system, shut down. This allows the brain to focus on the big picture—searching for the source of the threat, leaving smaller details unaddressed.[14]

The presence of fear creates the famous "flight or fight" response. Humans, when confronted with a real or perceived threat, react with the strongest drive within their nature—the drive to survive. When the intensity of the moment reaches its peak, the options for the person in the crosshairs narrows dramatically—either find a way out or find a way to win—flight or fight. The possibility of paralysis increases when neither option seems possible or when the circumstances eliminate the possibility of responding at all. In such cases, the person feels victimized and helpless.

In response to Jesus' instructions, the disciples were trying to make their way back across the Sea of Galilee. Nevertheless, obedience did not result in a carefree excursion. As the waves pounded against their craft and the winds impeded their progress, the reality of the situation undoubtedly dominated their thinking. They had no place to go and no way of escape. Their ability to fight the storm was diminishing; their best efforts were proving insufficient in the face of the threat. Progress became questionable as the superiority of the elements over human strength became evident. Furthermore, each individual might have experienced some of the physical and psychological responses to fear. Undoubtedly, the disciples faced tension, anxiety, and uncertainty.

How should we face fear? Jesus offers the antidote for fear—something that lends perspective and empowers persistence. As

---

14 Julia Layton, "How Fear Works," accessed March 19, 2017, http://science. howstuffworks.com/life/inside-the-mind/emotions /fear2.htm.

the disciples gathered in the Upper Room to celebrate the Passover, Jesus revealed the antidote. He reminded them of key kingdom principles and reiterated some of His previous teachings. He also gave them a new commandment: ***"Love one another. As I have loved you, so you must love one another"*** (John 13:34).[15] During this gathering, Jesus announced His departure and attempted to prepare them for what was about to take place: ***"Let not your heart be troubled; believe in God, believe also in Me"*** (John 14:1). At the risk of over-simplifying, I would suggest that Jesus gave more than a word of encouragement. I believe Jesus gave us a solution. We can counteract fear with faith—not mere faith in something, but faith in God.

Faith tends to be a rather tricky concept or something rather ambiguous. Believe what? Believe that because you will want it, it will come to pass? Believe in your ability to do it, therefore you will? Believe that someone from somewhere will show up and make the difference? Believe that because you believe, your faith opens the door to the miraculous? Believe that your positive thought, energy, or confession will change circumstances and yield a favorable outcome? No, our Lord specifically identified the foundation of faith: ***"Believe in God, believe also in Me"*** (Jesus Christ, the Lord) (John 14:1).

The writer of the book of Hebrews declares, ***"And without faith it is impossible to please Him, for he who come to God must believe that He is, and that He is a rewarder of those who seek Him"*** (Hebrews 11:6). Faith begins by believing that God exists and He will reward those who pursue Him. Believing that God is, sounds simple enough. Doesn't everyone believe in God? Yet regarding the common belief that God exists, one must ask, "Which God do we believe in?" Do we believe in the God revealed in Scripture or the one described in pop culture and social

---

[15] Some people propose that Jesus was restating the words of Leviticus 19:18 and emphasized that the disciples are to love others as they love themselves. Jesus referred to this as the second commandment, tied to the first, which was lifted from the *Shema* (Deuteronomy 6:4-5), and called them to "love the Lord your God with all your heart and with all your soul and with all your mind and with all your strength" (Mark 12:30). However, a second look reveals that Jesus was now calling them to love each other as He loved them, not as they loved themselves.

media? Faith in a false god holds no promise, according to God's Word. Understanding God to be the Supreme Being described and revealed in Holy Writ and placing your faith in that same God is the key to receiving from Him the promises of His Word and the provisions of heaven.

The second phase of biblical faith relates to possibilities afforded. This connects to a biblical understanding of God—not only who He is, but what He will do. In His awesomeness and holiness, God is gracious and kind, merciful, and benevolent. His love is limitless. His is grace without measure; His tenderness, sweet as a mother's touch; and His protection more secure than any earthly force can offer. Jesus said, ***"If you then, being evil, know how to give good gifts to your children, how much more shall your Father who is in heaven give what is good to those who ask Him!"*** (Matthew 7:11). He was comparing an earthly father's ability and proclivity to address the needs of his children compared to that of our Heavenly Father. When we come to God, believing Him to be the God revealed in Scripture and accepting His Son, Jesus Christ, as provision for our sins and the pathway to relationship with God, we are adopted as children into His family. We become "the rewarded" and receive the promised outcome as one who seeks Him.

Let me share a personal experience to illustrate. It was my privilege to serve as the last president of Bethany University (BU).[16] Margaret and I had been called upon to serve in an interim capacity as the board conducted a search for the next president. The school had faced financial difficulties for more than twenty-five years, with a growing deferred maintenance and a continually declining enrollment. During our six months of service as interim president, we made some positive progress and the board asked us to stay. We knew the realities; either we received a major miracle or we needed to deal with the harsh reality of bringing closure to the oldest school in our Fellowship. We experienced some small miracles and realized significant progress in a few areas. The hand of God was evident on numerous

---

[16] Initially Glad Tidings Bible Institute, then Bethany Bible College, then Bethany College, and finally Bethany University.

occasions. Yet, in March 2011, a motion was presented at the District Council of the Northern California and Nevada District of the Assemblies of God to close the school.[17] People responded graciously and with generous giving. The funds raised at that event literally kept the school afloat through the end of the term. Students had fasted and prayed to see God spare BU.

During that council, we received a letter of intent to gift the school several million dollars, and the anticipation began. We celebrated a joyous graduation day and continued to plan and move forward. We were in the process of building a new cafeteria,[18] and worked to complete all the contingencies laid out in the letter of intent. As things unfolded, the person who promised the money withdrew his offer.[19] A few other funding possibilities arose, but those options quickly faded. In June, the district made the decision to close the 92-year-old institution. The final day was August 15, 2011. I confess, this was, without doubt, one of my biggest disappointments.

During those last months, God gave me a phrase, a definition of faith, which I often quoted and offer here: Faith is not a bargaining chip with which we can get whatever we want from God, but rather it is a resting place in which we can reside with confidence when we don't get what we want from God. I have long believed it takes more faith to trust God when He does not meet our expectations than when God fulfills our desires. The process is not based on my ability to impress God—if He is sufficiently impressed, I am rewarded. No! Faith means believing that God is and He is the rewarder of those who seek Him. However, the timing and substance of that reward may be far different from what was originally expected. This is the kind of faith, however, that flies in the face of fear and brings courage, strength, hope, and contentment.

---

[17] The churches of the district owned the school.

[18] The old cafeteria had burned down the previous summer. We had turned the chapel into a temporary cafeteria and the performing arts theater served as our chapel.

[19] We discovered the individual had no funds with which to fulfill the promise; all in all, it was a hoax.

The next question focuses on what happens to fear in the process. Usually, by focusing on the Father rather than the circumstances, insecurity is exchanged for security as God's child experiences a peaceful confidence that truly is unexplainable. The prophet Isaiah wrote: ***"The steadfast mind Thou wilt keep in perfect peace, because he trusts in Thee"*** (Isaiah 26:3). The Apostle Paul admonishes: ***"Be anxious for nothing, but in everything by prayer and supplication with thanksgiving, let your requests be made known to God. And the peace of God which surpasses all comprehension shall guard your hearts and your minds in Christ Jesus"*** (Philippians 4:6, 7). Replacing fear with faith facilitates a brand new ballgame. Now, instead of feeling like a hopeless victim, we begin to see the possibility of winning, rising above the circumstances, and successfully overcoming the storm.

How much faith is needed? Jesus described mustard seed faith (Matthew 17:20). The trick is to quit evaluating the amount of faith we have and make the decision to invest it all in the one recipient worthy of our faith. And again, this is not a figure of myths and fables; this is not a hero of folklore and urban legends. This is the God of history, the God of the Bible, the God of heaven and earth. Your faith in Him releases His power and His presence. Even before the wind dies down and the surf calms, the mind begins to relax and the heart feels secure. We begin to see that God is in control, not the storm or the circumstances. Stay in the boat, keep rowing, overcome that fear, and "sail on."

CHAPTER 6

The Fatigue Factor

The Apostle Paul wrote, *"And let us not lose heart in doing good, for in due time we shall reap if we do not grow weary"* (Galatians 6:9). Growing weary is a reality of life. Ostensibly, the propensity knows no boundaries, from first century Christians in Galatia to twenty-first century believers from who-knows-where. A simple passage of Scripture provides a final proof of the overall impact of weariness. The encounter between Jesus and an un-named woman serves as the backdrop for a well-known story. John gives us the description: *"So He came to a city of Samaria, called Sychar, near the parcel of ground that Jacob gave to his son Joseph; and Jacob's well was there. Jesus therefore being wearied from His journey, was sitting thus by the well. It was about the sixth hour"* (John 4:5, 6). Yes, that's right! Jesus, living in a human body and dealing with life from our vantage point, grew weary.

Weariness stems from a multiplicity of sources. The common understanding of the word suggests being physically or mentally exhausted due to hard work, exertion, or strain. Jesus, feeling heat from the religious hierarchy, made His way from Judea toward Galilee. Normally, this would be a longer trek than the path Jesus chose. Jews did not travel through Samaria, the region lying between His previous location and His desired destination. The prejudice was deep, reaching back to the days of the Assyrians who had defeated Israel. Simply stated, the people from the ten northern tribes were displaced and a new race developed from intermarriage. The people became known as Samaritans and the Jews disenfranchised these people. The animosity between "the cousins" was well-known and deep seated. Jesus, however, did not take the usual route around Samaria; He chose to go through the forbidden territory. John's Gospel states: *"And He __had to pass through Samaria"__* (John 4:4 underlining added). I do not believe this was merely a comment regarding direction, but rather an indication of a divine appointment. He was not merely taking the shortest route, He was moving in the will of the Father for eternal purposes.

Ostensibly fatigued from His journey, Jesus sat down at the well. To restate the obvious, our Lord knew weariness and fatigue as He experienced life as a human. This was a necessary piece of the Father's plan. As previously stated, not only was Jesus to be our Savior, but also a High Priest who would stand in the courts of heaven on our behalf. As the writer of Hebrews declares, *"For we do not have a high priest who cannot sympathize with our weaknesses, but one who has been tempted in all things as we are, yet without sin"* (Hebrews 4:15). Our Lord did not experience some symbolic existence on our planet, totally protected and isolated from the diseases, difficulties, disappointments, and dilemmas known by the rest of humanity. Jesus knew firsthand the struggles of the flesh, including weariness and fatigue.

In like manner, the disciples were at a point of exhaustion when they headed across the Sea of Galilee. The Scripture describes their weariness and need for rest prior to their encounter with the crowd and the day of ministry provided by Jesus. You will recall Mark's words: *"For there were many people coming and going, and they did not even have time to eat"* (Mark 6:31). Remember, Jesus had suggested that they cross the Sea of Galilee (prior to the feeding of the 5,000) to get away from the press of ministry, affording some time to themselves. The news of the death of John the Baptist and the demands associated with continually meeting people's needs had taken a toll. The anticipation of a respite was never realized and could have led to disappointment and provided additional reason for the fatigue factor.

As the sun set and the responsibilities waned, the tired dozen began their journey to Bethsaida. Their weariness was soon exacerbated. The disciples found themselves battling the elements—not only struggling to make progress, but simply trying to stay upright on the sea. Although we do not know the exact time when they embarked on the journey, we can only assume that they had worked their way across the water for 4-6 hours. Matthew's account indicates it was the fourth watch when Jesus reached them (Matthew 14:25). This places the time somewhere between 3:00 and 6:00 a.m. John's Gospel states that they had rowed three or four miles (John 6:19). Having physically powered my 12-foot aluminum boat across a lake with a strong breeze in my face, I can only imagine the energy expended in their efforts to row a craft large enough to carry twelve men through a full-blown storm. To say they were exhausted after that many hours, rowing that distance, under the circumstances they faced, might just be an understatement.

As previously mentioned, Mark's Gospel explains that Jesus had suggested their initial trip across the sea: ***"And He said to them, 'Come away by yourselves to a lonely place and rest a while'"*** (Mark 6:32). Fred Grieve, a professor at Bethany Bible College, paraphrased the passage with a contemporary bent that gave practical application. He was well-known for saying, "Come apart before you come apart."[20] This simple encouragement becomes more than a nice idea.

The experience of the disciples came to a satisfactory ending. However, living under the pressure of constant demands and heavy responsibilities can place a person in danger of moving past fatigue to burnout, if simple, yet strategic steps, are not taken. Though other professions undoubtedly can be characterized with the same potential, the ministry can leave even a strong person ragged. Archibald D. Hart writes: "Pastors tend to become overly involved emotionally, overextend themselves, and then feel overwhelmed by the emotional demands imposed by others. And the more people there are to feel responsible for, the greater the opportunity for burnout." He further explains, "Theorizing does not help us appreciate how destructive and debilitating caring for others can be. The pastor, who was once vibrant with power and enthusiasm, able to motivate others to service and godly living, and given to caring and concern, becomes reduced

---

[20] Fred Grieve spoke these words often in class. He would later become a professor at Southern California College (later known as Vanguard University). Bethany Bible College would become Bethany College and then Bethany University.

to useless ineffective rubble, emotionally exhausted, and deeply fearful."[21]

Burnout need not be interminable. Furthermore, it can be avoided. Dealing appropriately and correctly with fatigue will help. Let's review some simple, yet often ignored, factors regarding fatigue.

1. *Recognize the reality.* Everyone gets tired; it is part of having a busy and deliberate life, accomplishing tasks, and realizing goals. It should not be viewed as a sign of weakness, though, at times, it can serve as an indicator of less than best practices when it comes to schedule and commitment.

2. *Regular rest is a necessity, not just a suggestion.* God did not create us to run endlessly ignoring the need for rest and recharging. God rested on the seventh day, not because He needed the rest, but because He was establishing a pattern for us to follow. He instituted the concept of Sabbath long before Adam and Eve's disobedience and dismissal from the Garden. In other words, the need for rest is not the result of the Fall; it was a created norm. Too often, we view the Sabbath as an Old Testament restriction rather than as a timeless principle. Admittedly the Pharisees added many demands and regulations regarding the observance of the seventh day, which hold no application for today. However, the Ten Commandments are viewed as God's desire for His people throughout all the ages.

   Keep in mind that God instituted the Sabbath as a day of rest as opposed to a day of worship. Some scholars have even suggested that the Israelites, to whom the Decalogue was originally delivered, established the seventh day as a day of worship, as opposed to it being a part of

---

21 Archibald D. Hart, "Depressed, Stressed and Burnt Out: What's Going on in My Life?" *Enrichment Journal*, accessed March 22, 2017, http://enrichment journal.ag.org/200603/200603_020_burnout.cfm.

the directive. Biblical understanding seems to support the idea that every day is a day of worship and every aspect of our existence is an expression of worship. No doubt, times of coming together for the purpose of joint exaltation of our God, instruction from His Word, and encouragement are not only beneficial, but biblically instructed (Hebrews 10:25). New Testament believers, by and large, celebrated joint worship on the first day of the week in honor and recognition of resurrection day. Wisdom would suggest that individuals responsible for or heavily involved in Sunday celebrations and services set aside a different day for rest and recuperation.

Taking a day off is not the unpardonable sin and should be a scheduled and routinely practiced habit. The Messianic Complex tends to infect a good percentage of ministers, as well as other individuals in helping professions. Being "the hero" can become addictive. The adrenaline rush resulting from the thanks and praise one might receive creates an appetite for more. The compassion that once fueled a sense of total commitment can be replaced by an egocentric sense of self-importance that refuses to rest or even admit the need for rest.

However, rest must be experienced more frequently than one day a week. "Sleep is not a luxury," says James O'Brien, medical director of the Boston SleepCare Center in Waltham, Massachusetts, "It's a necessity for optimal functioning."[22] It is generally accepted that 7-8 hours of sleep is advisable. Too often, individuals ignore the recommendations, feeling they are exempt. Some augment their night time rest with power naps, though others find the practice more detrimental than beneficial. The inability to receive adequate sleep may be a sign of other problems that need attention. Sleep apnea, medical conditions, medications, stimulants, and life style issues (i.e., smoking, alcohol) will negatively affect one's ability to receive

---

[22] Anne Field, "Why Sleep is so Important," accessed September 18, 2017, https://hbr.org/2009/01/why-sleep-is-so-important.html.

adequate rest. Usually a good night's rest works wonders. The use of a sleep aid should not be considered improper. A number of highly recommended over-the-counter remedies exist that demonstrate few, if any, side effects.

3. *Good nutrition.* Diet is a contributing factor to a person's well-being. Eating with good nutrition in mind will facilitate health and wholeness while eating fatty foods causes one to feel lethargic. The President's Council on Fitness, Sports, and Nutrition states: "The link between good nutrition and healthy weight, reduced chronic disease risk, and overall health is too important to ignore. By taking steps to eat healthy, you'll be on your way to getting the nutrients your body needs to stay healthy, active, and strong."[23] Research shows that a lack of vitamin B12 and vitamin D can also contribute to prolonged weariness and fatigue.[24] Good eating habits will help restore these much needed provisions. Poor eating habits can also contribute to health issues associated with a continual sense of tiredness, especially for individuals with diabetes.

4. *Exercise, recreational activities, and hobbies.* Taking adequate time to recuperate, refresh, reflect, and refuel on a regular basis recharges the batteries and renews the mind. Exercise, recreation, hobbies, interaction with other people, and taking time to escape the pressure are activities that contribute to rejuvenation and help prevent chronic fatigue. These activities can also contribute to a better night's sleep, as they help relieve the mind of stress and create a sense of physical relaxation. Research has

---

[23] U.S. Department of Health and Human Services, "Importance of Good Nutrition," accessed November 8, 2017, https://www.hhs.gov/fitness/eat-healthy/importance-of-good-nutrition/index.html.

[24] Eleni N. Gage, "Are You Tired All the Time," Real Simple, accessed November 8, 2017, https://www.realsimple.com/health/preventative-health/sleep/tired-all-time

shown that even light levels of exercise improve sleep quality.[25]

5. *Create a conducive environment.* Rest is best experienced when certain elements are in place. Establishing a regular schedule for daily activities, including a routine bed time, prove beneficial. Going to bed at approximately the same time sets one's body clock. Eliminating stimulation—whether emotional, mental, or physical—will contribute to the ability to rest and sleep. Reducing the amount of light in the room, regulating the temperature to a cooler setting, and using a comfortable and supportive mattress and pillow also contribute to increased rest.[26]

Not all required rest can be realized physically. Jesus said, ***"Come to Me, all who are weary and heavy-laden, and I will give you rest. Take My yoke upon you, and learn from Me, for I am gentle and humble in heart; and you shall find rest for your souls. For My yoke is easy, and My load is light"*** (Matthew 11:28-30). At times, the weariness represents more than a need for rest. The deflation of one's spirit and depletion of one's motivation leaves one incapable of finding solutions. Counseling may be required. However, a visit with the Wonderful Counselor always guarantees evident benefits. Finding a place—a quiet place—to be shut in with the Lord for prayer, reading His Word, journaling, and meditating creates an atmosphere for the Great Physician to bring healing and renewal.

Note, Jesus described His yoke as easy and His load as light. This reveals an important principle. If the yoke seems continually troublesome and the burden unusually heavy, possibly one has assumed responsibilities, which were not divinely ordained. Maybe the weight being carried has been acquired somewhere other than at the feet of Jesus. Delegation of responsibilities,

---

[25] The New York Times, "The Cure for Exhaustion?" accessed May 29, 2018, https://www.realsimple.com/health/preventative-health/sleep/tired-all-time.

[26] National Sleep Foundation, "Healthy Sleep Tips," accessed September 18, 2017, https://sleepfoundation.org/sleep-tools-tips/healthy-sleep-tips.

sharing the load of leadership, and accepting help will undoubt-edly assist. One should also consider utilizing tools and options not previously employed. Training others to grow their capacity is part of good leadership, but it will also help ease the load and lessen the stress on the leader. In so doing, we lessen the load on ourselves, while improving our capability to lead with energy, vision, and consistency.

Yes, we need to see the value of following these simple measures, but we must also understand the necessity of imple-menting these principles. A personal confession might be helpful. When writing my doctoral project, I would often try to hurry the process by spending long hours within a day trying to complete a chapter, finish some research, or rewrite a section. This push would often conclude in the wee hours of the morning, hours af-ter a long day at work. The next day, upon review of my late night and early morning contributions, I would end up eliminat-ing or deleting things. I would ask myself, "What was I thinking?" In this process, I learned that fatigue does not offer a good plat-form for good performance.

I have found that this principle also applies to manual labor! Oh! The mistakes I have made simply because I was too tired to do the job correctly. I must confess; when I am overly tired, I un-consciously bite the inside of my cheek. The resulting canker sore serves as a vivid reminder of the reality—fatigue can be harmful.

God's provisions and promises are ours for the asking and en-joying. However, God's desires us to obey and embrace His prin-ciples and precepts. Fatigue will happen, and sometimes we simply need to work through it. That's a fact. However, running on fumes will not allow you to complete your work satisfactorily or live a meaningful life. Rest is a *good* four-letter word.

CHAPTER 7

Motivation

Why do people do what they do? What motivates an individual to invest time, energy and/or resources? Identifying the reason a person begins, continues, and completes a task undoubtedly lends opportunity for better understanding of the individual, at least within the moment. So, why did the disciples leave Jesus alone on the shore and start making their way back across the sea—at night and over a body of water they knew to be less than predictable?

Motivation can arise from any number of different sources. A few common stimuli come to mind. At the risk of re-iterating a few already previously mentioned, I begin with the most common. Love motivates people. The love of a mother for her child, the love of a man for a woman, the deep affection of a patriot for his or her country, and the devotion of a disciple for the master/mentor all serve as examples. These relationships illustrate the incentive behind the sacrifices made, time given, chances taken, and total commitment displayed. Love truly fuels the passion and action taken by many people facing extraordinary situations, overcoming incredible odds. At the risk of presuming possible facts not in evidence, but presuming upon the nature of the twelve, I believe there was simply an element of love and respect for Jesus that gave release to an automatic response.

Fear is also a common motivator. Robert Evans Wilson Jr. suggests fear as the most powerful motivator.[27] This emotion stems from a number of possibilities: fear of death, fear of pain, disease, or injury, fear of failure, fear of being excluded or not

---

[27] Robert Evans Wilson Jr. "The Most Powerful Motivator: How Fear is Etched into Our Brain," posted September 23, 2009, accessed September 20, 2017, https://www.psychologytoday.com/blog/the-main-ingredient/200909/the-most-powerful-motivator.

being accepted, fear of losing or being cheated, and the fear of missing an opportunity, to list a few. Fear may also complicate a situation because people often feel paralyzed by the fear. In the face of danger, each individual makes the choice of whether to overcome the posing threat (fight) or to escape the pending danger (flight). Since the disciples could not escape the storm, it may have been fear that propelled them in their continued efforts to keep their boat afloat and reach the other shore.

Another effective stimulus is reward, whether intrinsic or extrinsic. Intrinsic benefits include praise and recognition, a feeling of acceptance, being appreciated, a sense of accomplishment, and knowing that one is doing something meaningful. Extrinsic perks are usually monetary, be it in the form of bonuses, gifts, stock options, raises, or increased benefits. Other forms of extrinsic motivation include promotions, new levels of involvement, or added privileges. Undoubtedly, the proverbial dangling carrot provides incentive, for both individuals and groups.

The opportunity for growth, development, and increased knowledge also provides motivation. Consider a child wanting to master a subject or a college student preparing for a career. The personal thrill of learning new things, gaining new understanding, and rising to a new level of competency and ability inspires and propels people through the challenges involved in the process.

Some people experience overwhelming peer pressure, which can move them to do what they might not do otherwise. At times, it literally prompts them to do what they really do not wish to do. While writing this book, one of the lead stories in the media focused on members of the sports world refusing to stand for the national anthem. It started within the ranks of the NFL, but spread on a minimal scale to baseball with the threat of the NBA to follow. Participants were protesting the reported mistreatment administered by police when dealing with people of color, primarily in the large inner city areas of our country. The rationale proposed the injustice gave reason for professional athletes to refuse to participate in a time honored tradition as Americans. It started with one black football player, but then spread to members of every professional football team taking a knee instead of taking a stand. Other members of said teams demonstrated in similar fashion to show their support of fellow team-mates. In a short matter of time it became evident that some of the players did not know the right thing to do, but felt pressure to support those who were passionate in the cause.

Most people can remember times when an election or choice was determined by a show of hands. Any number of participants may have shown support for a candidate or option really not their preferred choice, but they did not want to be the only hand among their peers not raised to go along with the majority. This simple imagery serves as a prudent reminder that because a majority may rule, does not mean the majority is right. But I digress.

Anger can be a motivational factor as well. One can only estimate the number of reactions that have taken place, leaving death and bloodshed in the wake, purely based on the anger of an individual or group. Logic seems completely discarded as the outrage fostered by the memory of an injustice, assault, or total neglect becomes unleashed. Strangely enough, at times, the vengeance manifests itself toward people unknown to the assailant and fully innocent of any connection with the offense. Thus, the irrational dominates the moment and steers the mind and body to do what it would undoubtedly otherwise not do.

Desperation moves people into action. From hunger to the threat of losing one's home, desperate people have been known to take desperate measures. When listlessness and lethargy are tossed aside, people move in the pursuit of possibilities envisioned, whether or not they be realistic. This can lead—as in the case of anger, fear, and a number of other motivational stimuli—to negative outcomes as much as positive possibilities. However, I firmly believe in a simple principle: desperation is the seedbed for the miraculous. Let me explain.

When people are backed against the wall and have no alternatives, reliance on God and total commitment to prayer and faith may well release divine intervention otherwise unknown. Though we live in a day and culture of entitlement, the principle is not a part of the fabric that makes up the Kingdom of God. God does not interrupt situations to save us from our circumstances and the frustrations of our own attempts to resolve the problem. Yes, the Father knows what we have need of before we ask (Matthew 6:8) but, at times, He waits until we ask for His help. Why?

A wise parent comes to know the necessity of allowing the child to endure hardship, to struggle with problems, and even experience the fallacy of self-prescribed solutions. An even wiser God understands we will only learn certain principles the hard way. At times, we will only move out of our immaturity when forced to do so. He wants us to grow up. This means facing the reality that we cannot do things for ourselves. It also lends the possibility of having to admit our dependency on the Almighty. That sense of helplessness, that sense of desperation will often result in making room for a miracle to take place. Something we never would have experienced on our own becomes a reality because we set aside our own resources and strategies—knowing none would suffice— and reach out to the Lord. Desperation might be called the motivation that releases the miraculous.

As the disciples began their trek back across the Sea of Galilee, logic seems to indicate the immediate response arose out of a simple sense of obedience to the Savior's instructions. The Scripture states that Jesus *"made the disciples get into the boat"* (Matthew 14:22; cf. Mark 6:45). Love for Christ and a learned trust in His voice and direction made their compliance an easy decision. That assumption comes from the believed legitimacy of the triangle described earlier regarding comprehending obedience: love, trust, obedience. Exactly when each man had gained a sense of love and affection for Christ remains unknown. It would seem impossible to gauge exactly what caused them to leave their former occupations, lifestyles, and relationships to walk in the footsteps of the Master. Trust undoubtedly was learned as the result of their faith that He was the fulfillment of Old Testament prophecy, but also firsthand testimony to His teachings, His dealings with people, and His proven trustworthiness. Consequently, upon hearing His voice, they began the voyage back across the Sea of Galilee.

Interestingly, the disciples started across the Sea without Jesus; He stayed behind. They did not express hesitancy in their response; they simply went back to the boat and began the journey into the encroaching darkness and embraced the challenges of the sea. Could this not speak to another possible motivation? Is it possible that their frustration and fatigue induced their behavior? The prospect of rowing back across the sea may have been less than a preferred activity, considering all they had experienced. However, viewing the possible end of this whole experience may well have provided energy and stimulation to heartily embrace the instructions.

The day had begun with the prospect of relaxation and a welcomed interlude. However, those expectations would remain unrealized. Their arrival in Bethsaida brought re-engagement with ministry as the crowd gathered and the Lord resumed His normal response to the peoples' needs and the opportunity for ministry. By the end of the day, the chosen twelve may have felt something other than a mere compulsion to comply with the Lord's directive. They could bring an end to this uninvited interruption in their plans. The trip back across this unpredictable body of water, at night, may well have seemed like their best option at the time.

As time progressed and the situation grew nearly impossible, that same sense of a potential conclusion may well have motivated them to keep rowing, to keep trying. The thought that something not really enjoyable may soon come to an end can motivate a person to continue and see it through. Admittedly, that may seem strange at first consideration, yet experience would prove the same true. From a tough workout in the gym to a miserable chore that needs completion, the hope that arises due to the simple consideration of the end-in-sight, spurs renewed energy and determination.

Obedience may well incorporate loyalty, possibly love, and even a sense of obligation. The disciples had left their former lives to follow Jesus. By biblical account, most seem to have been instantaneous in their decision to do so. Something drew them. Something convinced grown men, locked into career paths, to abandon previous plans and desires to adopt new lifestyles and priorities. Undoubtedly, the words and the miracles they observed firsthand confirmed their decisions. This was the fulfillment of the Old Testament prophets! This was the Christ, the Son of the Living God, as Peter had confessed (Matthew 16:16). That sense of reality brought about love and trust from these select followers, which translated to a commitment, lived out through obedience. I believe this was the initial motivation that took the disciples from the shore to the oars. I confess my suspicion, however, that the disciples were also driven by their desire to see this whole experience come to an end, although they became absorbed by desperation as the situation changed and they found themselves in a fight to survive.

As I consider the disciples' motivations and reflect on the whole matter of motivation, I confess my own contemplation as to what drives me to do certain things. Admittedly, over-analysis can prove to be counterproductive. The discovery of every motive for every facet of one's life simply is not necessary or beneficial. We do some things out of habit. We do some things because we were taught to do them. The performance of certain tasks comes as the result of being a human being, while other things are performed as the result of feeling some sense of responsibility. I can honestly say I have done some things simply because I felt I had to do them. I felt obligated. Admittedly, there were times I began to feel some sense of satisfaction and possibly even gratification in the process of functioning in less than attractive duties. Every job or involvement contains the element of stimulus, whether positive or negative. The discovery of the same may seem important at times; nonetheless, knowing why we do what we do may not be critical most of the time. However, personal evaluation of the *why* helps understand the *who*. Who I truly am becomes a little clearer when I understand why I do what I do.

One of the duties as a minister incorporated traveling to care facilities, commonly called "rest homes." The resistance did not come from a lack of affection or appreciation for the elderly, because I dearly love old people. (I am one!) The task was odious because the conditions were less than inviting: the smells, the sights, at times the attitudes of staff, the obvious loneliness, and detectable neglect. Mental preparation became a required process for the performance of this simple duty. Oh, other staff members were willing to go, and for more than two decades of ministry, I had other pastors assigned this responsibility. However, there were times when I needed to go; my presence was important. Usually, as previously mentioned, I would find myself walking away from a facility smiling, feeling grateful for the encounter(s) just experienced. Initially, however, obligation was the driving force.

Other aspects of my job were obligatory, but I found my motivation from a much more positive source. For example, preaching. I love to preach! Though some would assume this a given, there was a time in my life when I felt much differently. I think there was just something about being a "preacher" that truly bothered me. When people asked me about my plans and if the ministry was in my future, I would commonly respond, "I don't have to preach, I have talent." Whoa! Well, through a series of events and circumstances—unquestionably orchestrated by the Lord—I came to a point of recognizing the fallacy of my prejudice and accepted God's call. Now, please understand, the opportunity to stand in public and speak has never been considered a deplorable possibility. Some people might even suggest that if I was going to be in church, I was going to be the guy talking. Please don't allow that revelation to diminish your estimation of my divine appointment. However, spending the time necessary to study and prepare for three or four sermons and/or teachings per week seemed less than inviting. But as much as I am confident in my calling, I am also convinced of God's subsequent transformation within me. Today, the preparation provides nearly as much delight as the actual presentation. Let me explain.

Following graduation from Bethany Bible College (later Bethany College and then Bethany University), I received my license to preach in 1968. Because of my aforementioned hesitancy to be the pontificating pulpiteer, I did not move forward to ordination for a decade. In our Fellowship, ordination, though not exclusively for preaching pastors, tends to indicate a commitment to that aspect of service. After progressing in ministry with an emphasis on music, Margaret and I recorded a long play album[28] in London, England. It was an incredible experience. We also decided it was time for me to move forward in the credentialing process, and I was ordained in 1978.

We traveled for approximately eighteen months, singing and preaching every weekend, working day jobs to "support my habit," as Margaret describes it. In 1980, the construction of houses

---

[28] For those of the younger generations, an album refers to a large vinyl record played at 33 1/3 speed.

was at a very low level and work was hard to find. I had been working in construction during this time frame, but jobs were no longer available. While my wife worked, I spent several months reading Jeremiah over and over. I was trying to figure out what God was doing to me.

We decided that maybe I should create a resume and consider pastoring a church. I applied to three churches, as my memory serves. One of them was in Medford, Oregon. My good friend, Ormel Chapin—former college roommate and best man at our wedding—served as the youth director for the Oregon District Council of the Assemblies of God. He had been gracious to invite us to minister at a few youth camps and continually encouraged me in my development and growth of expression. Upon hearing of my decision to pastor, Orm called and suggested this perfect opportunity. Within weeks, we were the new pastors at Bethel Church. What a blast! We experienced nearly five years of continued growth and fulfillment. I thoroughly enjoyed the challenges. My attitudes were totally altered and preaching became a passion. Returning to the educational arena, I earned a Master's Degree from the Assemblies of God Theological Seminary. I was a "word man." Although I faced a vast array of responsibilities with a growing congregation (growing from 75 people to 500 in those five years), preaching became the focus. I am still grateful for the patient congregation who allowed me to grow into the role. Now, more than 35 years later, I still confess my love of preaching. Occasional opportunities to apply my craft are afforded and are relished indeed.

What was my motivation? Was it to be in front, to be heard, or to wow the crowd with a turn of phrase? Did I find it satisfying to present some little known fact? Was it the gratification of knowing that I had held the audience captive with a mesmerizing story, the near harmonic flow of well-orchestrated alliteration, or the perfectly timed humorous antidote? Did I merely revel in the attention? Had I become addicted to the "on stage" rush and exhilaration? Or, was I feeling the sense of fulfillment in doing what God called and created me to do? I choose to believe it was the later, though there were undoubtedly times that the purity of my motives may have been compromised.

One of the things I truly enjoyed during our years of ministry was doing radio programs. I had been introduced to the process while serving as a minister of music in Roseville, California, our last place of staff ministry before moving up to the big time. The lead pastor and I shared in the creation of a radio program that aired weekly. I was responsible for putting together the musical selections, while he hosted the show and provided biblical commentary and inspiration.

In Medford, a parishioner, who would later become my first youth pastor, was a true professional in the radio industry. He assisted me in the creation of a similar type of program and taught me much about the technical aspects of production. I followed the same course in Albany, where we pastored for more than twenty-two years. I learned to engineer the process and found a great deal of joy in sitting behind the microphone, directing, and producing the "theater of the mind."

As time progressed, our church sponsored two weekly programs. One program provided a basic music and comment-driven piece while the second presented reduced versions of Sunday sermons. During the early 2000s, budget restraints called for the reduction of expenditures and the church board decided to nix the radio broadcasts. I was heartbroken. What about all of those listeners out there? We were diminishing our spiritual impact on the community. My ability to influence the thinking and moral fabric of the surrounding towns was becoming severely limited. I was not happy about the decision.

A lone letter arrived to express disappointment for the lack of our radio presence: one letter! A few friends mentioned—over time—that they missed hearing my voice on the Sunday morning broadcasts. Bottom line: the only person who really cared about the radio programs was me. Well, possibly, it would be better said, no one received more out of the broadcasts than I did. Going to the stations and recording the programs was a diversion in my week. It was fun sitting behind the microphone. It gave me opportunity to play a little different role. So, my motivation was not purely evangelism or outreach; it was a little more self-satisfying. Recording the radio programs gave me a chance to get out of the office, out of my routine, and "play DJ." I do not suggest this was necessarily a bad thing. Obtaining a sense of self-satisfaction and truly enjoying something that provides benefit to yourself and others cannot be a bad thing. However, honest evaluation reveals that my disappointment in the termination of that opportunity had been disguised as having purer motives.

Surely the disciples' motives were not as convoluted! However, the reason the disciples responded to the instructions to cross the Sea of Galilee may best be answered by my first response in chapter three: obedience. Why I do what I do may not be so simply described. Recognition of my motives, however, brings revelation of who I am—or who I was at the time—as well as an indication of my growth and development. It is not self-abasing if it leads to self-improvement, and that should be the goal.

CHAPTER 8

Feeling Alone

It is one thing to feel alone when you are, but it is quite another to feel alone even though you are with a group of people. Let's think about it for a moment—being alone and feeling alone. One represents position, the other identifies perspective. Multiple scenarios might be used to illustrate this difference. However, the disciples' mix of emotions and realities undoubtedly provided a more than adequate environment for feeling alone. Again, the story does not make reference to this factor, but I suggest it was a probable feeling at that moment. I propose that at least one disciple may have felt that they were rowing more deliberately, praying more effectively, and focused more intently on surviving the storm and reaching the shore than the rest. Although everyone may be participating, at some level, a person can literally feel all alone in the effort and in doing what needs to be done.

An Old Testament story comes to mind (1 Kings 18-19). Elijah, a significant prophetic figure in the ninth century B.C., served the northern kingdom of Israel by offering counsel, guidance, and warning to a nation, which had lost its spiritual bearings. As part of his attempt to draw the nation back into relationship with Jehovah, he challenged the prophets of Baal to a winner-takes-all battle on Mount Carmel. Elijah and the prophets of Baal built altars, prepared sacrifices, offered prayers, and agreed that the divine being who answered by fire would be seen as the true God.

The story becomes rather humorous, as Elijah belittles his opponents and their god. At the end of the day, the prophets of Baal had been destroyed. God not only answered by fire, but also with rain. God ended a three year draught through the prophet's prayer. Jezebel, the wife of King Ahab, took serious offense at the man of God's demonstration. She promised to take his life in exchange for the prophets of Baal he had killed. Elijah, strong in faith and confidence on Mount Carmel, ran like a scared child, obviously knowing the cruelty and wickedness of the queen. After leaving his servant in Beersheba, Elijah entered the wilderness alone and sat down under a juniper tree and bemoaned his very existence. Elijah felt alone. Now, admittedly, he was alone at this point and time, but his expression really had nothing to do with his lack of companionship. Remember, he had left his servant by choice.

God provided him an extraordinary meal that provided sustenance for forty days and nights. Then the Lord asked the prophet, "What are you doing here, Elijah?" His response lends insight into his state of mind. *"I have been very zealous for the Lord, the God of Hosts; for the sons of Israel have forsaken your covenant, torn down your altars and killed your prophets with the sword. And I alone am left, and they seek my life, to take it away"* (1 Kings 19: 9, 10). He repeated the same words later in the story.

Truth be known, thousands of people had not betrayed their allegiance to the Lord. Nevertheless, Elijah felt alone. Physically, he was alone—that was his position. More importantly, he felt alone—a reflection of his perspective. Jezebel was no ordinary foe, and her threats were never empty. One need only read the story in 1 Kings 21 to understand Elijah's fear. Ahab, Jezebel's husband, wanted a particular vineyard. Naboth, the owner, refused to sell his property, so Jezebel plotted Naboth's death and made a way to satisfy King Ahab's desire. She was not a lady to be taken lightly. Elijah had good reason to run, and feeling alone in that moment was highly justified.

At times, Jesus found himself alone. The story under scrutiny reveals one of those moments. After the disciples departed and Jesus had sent the multitude away, the Scripture tells us, *"He was there alone"* (Matthew 14:23).[29] John 6:16 gives a little more insight: *"Jesus therefore perceiving that they were intending to come and take Him by force to make Him king, withdrew again to the mountain by Himself alone."* At this juncture, one must understand the mission of the Master. He had not come to fulfill mankind's desires. He did not enter our realm to make a

---

[29] Also, see Mark 6:47.

name for himself. His incarnation served one primary goal: to provide the perfect sacrifice for the sins committed by His prized creation. The people heard His words, received the provisions of the miracles, waited anxiously to experience His healing touch, and sincerely believed that He had come from God. No other person had ever provided so much to so many people in such a short period of time. Why would they not want to make him king? But, that was not why He had come. The people to whom He had come could not understand His perspective. They saw monarch potential in the Master. In the knowledge of the divine will of the Father and the eternal plan, Jesus was the only one who knew the totality of the story.

As the ministry of our Lord was about to unfold, He found himself alone in the wilderness for forty days and nights. Completing the preparation ordained by the Father, He was tempted by the devil—again, finding himself alone. The night before His crucifixion, He led the disciples from the Upper Room to the Garden of Gethsemane. Leaving the three disciples who had drawn closest to Him, Jesus proceeded a little further, desiring to deal with the implications of the moment in private conversation with the Father. After agonizing in prayer, He returned to the disciples to find them asleep. He encouraged them to watch and pray, returning to His intense and intimate communion with God. A second and third check on Peter, James, and John revealed their return to slumber. Truly Jesus was alone—physically, emotionally, and spiritually.

The cross affords another snapshot of Christ's sense of being alone. The mocking crowd stood below Him while the Roman soldiers fulfilled their responsibilities, untouched by the events. A few of the women who had come to believe in Jesus and followed Him, stood in horror as they watched His life ebb away. John, the brother of James, was the only one of the twelve disciples identified as being present on that historic hillside. Conversations between Christ and the people at the crucifixion were minimal; Jesus primarily communicated with His Father. In His dying moments, Jesus cried with a loud voice, ***"'Eli, Eli, lama sabachthani?' That is, 'My God, My God, why hast Thou forsaken Me?'"*** (Matthew 27:46). The Creator of the universe undisputedly felt all alone!

In the creation story, the Lord concluded, *"It is not good for the man to be alone"* (Genesis 2:18). Although the first man enjoyed the companionship of various forms of birds and animals, he was not complete without the creation of woman, which God fashioned to be complimentary to Adam. God's conclusion was not merely an expressed reason for the creation of a woman or a proposal for marriage. God knew Adam needed to be in a relationship where he became part of something bigger than himself. The author of Ecclesiastes states, *"Two are better than one because they have a good return for their labor. For if either of them falls, the one will lift up his companion. But woe to the one who falls when there is not another to lift him up"* (Ecclesiastes 4:9, 10). The obvious speaks loudly: being alone has its disadvantageous.

On the other hand, there are times when being alone can be a blessing or the perfect situation for the moment. As I have aged, I appreciate time alone. During my younger years, I had to have people around me all the time. I hated being alone, except during periods when I was feeling sorry for myself. On such occasions, I didn't believe anyone understood what I was feeling or, worse yet, didn't understand me. As I progressed in life and ministry, time alone became essential for my effectiveness and, at times, for mere survival. I needed time to think, reflect, dream, pray, study, write, and prepare. To this day, I enjoy time in quiet reflection, deep thought, and contemplation. Furthermore, when time alone seems unavailable, I become somewhat frustrated. I am hesitant to assume this new appreciation came as a matter of maturity, as I sometimes wonder if my personality has morphed over time. Nevertheless, I do understand not everyone enjoys being alone. In fact, for some people it is more than uncomfortable and can become life-threatening. Psychologist Kendra Cherry lists a number of attention-grabbing negative effects of being alone: (1) depression and suicide, (2) cardiovascular disease and stroke, (3) increased stress levels, (4) decreased memory and learning, (5) antisocial behavior, (6) poor decision-making, (7) alcoholism and drug abuse, (8) the progression of Alzheimer's disease, and (9) altered brain function.[30] Obviously, all of the above symptoms support the God-initiated conclusion that it is not good for man (or woman) to be alone.

Individuals on two extremes of the spectrum struggle with being alone. First, individuals with a perfectionist tendency (which often contributes to low self-esteem) may tend to be self-degrading, self-punishing, and self-destructive. When something goes wrong or when expectations are not realized, they blame the person in the mirror. Second, some individuals can feel over-ly confident regarding their abilities to solve personal problems and feel the best advice comes from within. All too often, these people tend to think they can beat their problems without any help from the outside. History and experience tend to prove, however, that they may well be their own worst counselors. In either case, the perfectionist or the self-sufficient person may find it detrimental to be alone.

The seventeenth century philosopher and scientist, Blaise Pascal, made an interesting statement: "All of humanity's prob-lems stem from man's inability to sit quietly in a room alone."[31] With that thought in mind, doctoral students at the University of Virginia conducted research to test the validity of Pascal's asser-tion. The study involved placing participants in a room for the purpose of simply considering their own thoughts for ten to twenty minutes. They were not allowed to take anything with them into their time of isolation—no cell phones, watches, iPods, computers, or electronic devices of any kind. Each person was shown a few photographs to help stimulate thought. If a person found it unbearable to be alone with their thoughts they could utilize a button that released an electric shock. Before the exper-iment began, each participant tested the button. Most partici-

---

[30] Kendra Cherry, "What You Should Know about Loneliness: Causes and Health Consequences of Feeling Lonely," updated February 22, 2018, accessed March 28, 2018, https://www.verywell.com/loneliness-causes-effects-and-treatments-2795749.

[31] Adam Wernick, "A New Study Found People are Terrible at Sitting Alone with their Thoughts. How about You?" posted July 19, 2014, accessed March 26, 2018, https://www.pri.org/stories/2014-07-19/new-study-found-people-are-terrible-sitting-alone-their-thoughts-how-about-you.

pants confessed a preference not to access the button again, as the result was unpleasant. Some stated they would pay money to avoid the experience again. Nevertheless, the research revealed that 70 percent of the males and 25 percent of the females pressed the button again.[32] Ostensibly, Pascal was correct, at least in a limited fashion. I'm not sure "all of humanity's problems stem" from this inability, though admittedly, we have become an activity-oriented culture (and possibly, world). Could it be we have reached a point where quiet thought and contemplation seem abnormal if not an experience to avoid?

One has to wonder why people choose to resist time alone, time to be quiet, reflect, think, postulate, recapitulate, and meditate. Could it be that when we are alone with our thoughts we find ourselves confronted with our inabilities, our failures, and even our seeming insignificance? We all face the possible negative impact derived from serious introspection. Our sins, our mistakes, and our inadequacies can loom large and in charge. Only masochistic mentalities would desire to revisit such an experience very often. However, when that honesty results in admission and true confession, we experience forgiveness and find freedom. Along with that divine provision, we received a renewed affirmation of His delight in us as His creation. With a resolved past and a renewed sense of His creative genius, we can freely, seriously, and with excitement ask: "What next?" Nothing pleases the Father more than a child considering all the possibilities—dreaming, searching, planning, challenging previous perceptions, considering new ventures, and making new discoveries. Such opportunities usually are not realized without being ostracized from the pressure, the people, and the problems. Some things do not happen without alone time. Suffice it to say, being alone can be beneficial for specific purposes and for limited periods of time. However, as a general rule, we need companionship. God created us as social creatures. Keep in mind that just being in a group does not automatically translate into being socially connected. Various circumstances—as already described—may

---

[32] Ibid.

contribute to lack of connection, even when in the company of other people.

Quite possibly our Lord anticipated this in the giving of the Great Commission: *"Go therefore and make disciples of all the nations, baptizing them in the name of the Father and the Son and the Holy Spirit, teaching them to observe all that I commanded you; and lo, I am with you always, even to the end of the age"* (Matthew 28:19, 20). Note the last line. In obeying the Lord's command, in dealing with life according to the priorities He has ordained, or in serving the Master with a whole heart, could it be that we will feel alone at times? Consequently, He made a promise: "I am with you always." We are never alone, though we may be alone. The promise of the angel when announcing the birth of the Savior to Joseph, has become the constant provision to all who believe: *"Emmanuel: God with us"* (Matthew 1:23). Denying our feelings and embracing our faith, we move into the situation, the dilemma, or the story of our lives with assurance that we are not alone. He is with us, even in the storm—especially in the storm.

On the other side of the coin, it seems important to address the fact that, at times, people contribute to their own loneliness. Through actions or attitudes found objectionable by others, an individual may find desired fellowship and companionship less likely. One common scenario stems from unforgiveness. Once a person decides to hold on to a grievance, the possibility of bitterness and even hatred may increase as time passes. Obviously, any contact with the party guilty of the offense becomes unthinkable. In addition, the offended person often chooses to reject contact with people who are friends of the disliked individual. The number of people included within that circle tends to increase as time progresses. The group of people who might want to spend time with the person also begins to shrink. Even close friends and family members may choose to keep their distance.

Anger is a common emotion, but all too often it becomes a harmful characteristic of a person's life. Sad but true, some people seem to be angry all the time. Whether connected to one critical moment or a string of experiences, rage becomes a realized response. The fire blazes quickly in reaction to a word spoken, an action taken, or an unexplainable stimulus. The location or environment does not seem to make any difference.

The world of golf provides numerous stories that illustrate uncontrolled anger. The memories of most golfers are replete with the unhappy occasion of being partnered with someone who threw a club after an errant shot. Numerous stories exist—some true, some urban legend—describing golfers who have literally hurt themselves or others as a result of a golf club becoming a missile. Watching an angry person slam a club into the ground, damage the green, or smash a piece of the golf cart, accompanied by a demonstration of foul language, truly takes a toll on the value of the attempt for a little recreation. Literally, I have identified individuals with whom I simply do not hold any desire to tee it up. More than likely, the golf course is not the only place where their anger is triggered and they embarrass themselves—and possibly hurt others. Angry people are not attractive!

Narcissistic people may find themselves walking alone. When every discussion, activity, or conversation must revolve around a particular person, companionship with other people may become difficult. Like individuals vexed with anger or filled with unforgiveness, the person displaying narcissistic behaviors remains in the dark. Others see what they do not see. In turn, they blame other people for the loneliness they experience, when obsession with self is the real reason people keep their distance.

Other emotional behaviors may also contribute to loneliness. As brutal as it may be to suggest, certain people just seem to drive people away. When feeling alone, wisdom would suggest we consider the possibility that we have created our own situation, inadvertently pushing people away. At the same time, we must recognize elements outside of our control.

Most people, despite their surroundings or attempts to fill the void, experience times when they feel alone. It is a reality of life. It also reminds us of the truth of God's conclusion in the Garden, which still rings clear: "It is not good for man (or woman) to be alone." At the risk of sounding idealistic, may I suggest that our feeling of being alone may be an unrecognized invitation to be alone with God. He is waiting.

CHAPTER 9

ABSORPTION TO THE POINT OF OBLIVION

Let's return to our story. In the midst of a life-threatening storm, the disciples see an image or person walking across the top of the water, coming toward them. No doubt it was dark, and the "creature" was at some distance from their boat. The Gospel writer indicates that they thought it was a ghost. Could things get any worse? Their obedience had been rewarded with a storm that had not only impeded their progress, but also threatened their survival. Fear had overwhelmed them, fatigue had taken its toll, and presumptuously personalities revealed individual weaknesses. Then, in a split-second, Jesus set them at ease, re-solved their tension and altered their perspective. Out of the murky fog came a revelation. The mystery was, in fact, a miracle, as the Lord Jesus approached them walking on the water. His voice provided the assurance they needed: ***"Take courage, it is I; do not be afraid"*** (Matthew 14:27).

Some might ask, "How could they not recognize the One they had walked with day after day, hearing His words, watching His movements, and knowing His ways? Here He is, walking on the water, and all they can fathom is the possibility of a ghost? How could that happen?" Jesus was doing something that defied the laws of physics, performing a feat not previously recorded in the annals of human history. They were so caught up in their own situation that they could not enjoy the moment or take in the wonder. Instead, they revolted against the reality and assumed the object to be an apparition. What possible explanation could there be?

Lest we waste time trying to lend explanation, a better in-vestment might be for us to consider how we might have re-sponded. Have we ever been blind to a miracle? Have we found ourselves in circumstances that so overwhelmed us or absorbed all our energies and focus that we did not see or understand what God was doing?

Focus is good. In fact, one of the primary factors of success involves a person's ability to concentrate, shutting out the non-essential for the sake of the critical. A simple illustration comes to mind. Some 35 years ago, while serving as lead pastor in Medford, Oregon, a mother brought her middle school-aged son to see me. He was a trombone player; I play trombone. Possibly she felt the shared musical interest would create a common ground. She was hoping her son might be willing to open up about some things and take some counsel from me. She explained he was doing very poorly in school. After an initial exchange, creating a level of comfort and establishing my desire to listen and see if I could help, he shared about his home and some of his struggles. He was the youngest of his siblings and his mom was the only parent at home. I quickly detected a sanguine personality, but no evidence of a rebellious spirit or unresolved anger. He shared his frustrations at school, and stated that maybe he just could not learn.

I told the young man I needed to finish a project and asked if he would be willing to give me a couple of minutes. I assigned him a little project: focus on a box of tissue positioned on the corner of my desk. He looked rather surprised and amused. I assured him it was important and proceeded to work on something unrelated to our appointment. The task at hand was really not important; it was a means to an end. After five minutes, I returned my attention to him. Taking the box from his view, I asked him to describe the object. He correctly identified the shape and major color on the container, but didn't have much else to offer as the result of the assignment.

Following a simple explanation on how to focus, we repeated the exercise. When given opportunity to describe the Kleenex box, he provided information I had not noticed. The lesson was learned. Grades improved and mom thought her pastor was a genius. Genius? No, but I had a simple awareness of a principle to be recognized and implemented: focus.

I confess, I have had a life-long desire to be an athlete. As a young man, the thought of playing second base for the New York Yankees served to fuel my passion for the game. I played baseball nearly every day during the summer. If there wasn't a game or practice, it was pepper in the back yard or batting rocks in the alley behind our house. I also played basketball and football, but being undersized, I found it easier to compete on the diamond. After college, I played softball for more than two decades. Admittedly, I didn't have the skill set to make it to the majors and had to refocus my energies during my high school years, but the memory lives and the story is still told.

One of the lessons learned from the diamond that has translated universally is the need to focus. Because you stand in the batter's box with a bat in your hand does not mean you are going to get a hit. Even with great skills and hand-eye coordination, success is not guaranteed without some serious concentration. Learning to pick up the spin on the ball, time the swing, and make good contact with the barrel of the bat are all critical elements of a batter's success at the plate. All of the above depend on focus. The batter must put aside the noise from the stands, the heckling of opposing players, the batter's plans after the game, or the events prior to the plate appearance. A divided attention will affect the player's capability and usually translates to a poorly hit ball or, worse yet, a strikeout.

Today, golf is my game of choice. Yes, it should be much easier to hit a ball sitting on a tee as opposed to one sailing through the air at 80-100 miles per hour. However, to presume automatic success would be silly and reveal a lack of knowledge regarding golf. The primary principle yielding success at the dish[33] remains the same for a flush shot on the links: focus.

In the course of life, immediate needs can capture our sense of attention to the point of skewing our sense of priority and conviction. The disciples were fixated on the storm and their survival. Their ability to see the One who could save them had been clouded, if not totally eliminated. It was more than a failure to recognize the familiar; it was a failure to focus on what was most important. The need to get beyond a current crisis is understandable, but being absorbed to the point of missing the so-

---

[33] Dish is a baseball term referring to home plate as the batter stands in ready to hit a pitch.

lution shows either a lack of focus or a severe case of misplaced focus.

Keep in mind the disciples were, in essence, doing nothing wrong; they were for all intents and purposes doing what was needed. Rowing was necessary. Hanging on to the boat when tossed by an oversized wave was totally understandable. Working together as a team in dealing with the turmoil surely speaks of a positive behavior. Furthermore, fighting through their fears in an attempt to survive and reach the shore equates to deserved admiration and commendation. However, the failure to recognize Jesus still tarnishes the disciples' reputation within the immediacy of this account.

The author of Hebrews lends profound and essential counsel for disciples of every generation as they face the elements of life—from the norm to the traumatic. Though the words read with a familiar ring, the application is far from automatic:

> *Therefore, since we have so great a cloud of witnesses surrounding us, let us also lay aside every encumbrance and the sin which so easily entangles us, and let us run with endurance the race that is set before us, fixing our eyes on Jesus, the author and perfecter of faith, who for the joy set before Him endured the cross, despising the shame, and has sat down at the right hand of the throne of God* (Hebrews 12:1, 2).

Although a series of sermons springs to mind from this passage, one phrase captures attention for this setting: "fixing our eyes on Jesus." This simple principle would obviously take on a whole new meaning for Peter, as well as the other disciples, as their time of discipleship continued. I would suggest, however, the phrase holds a secret for success for every pilgrim desiring to maintain progress, let alone survive life's storms.

Understanding a concept and being able to implement it is quite different. In the midst of the storm, focusing on something that seems far away as opposed to what is in your face provides a challenge, to say the least. The feel of the wind and the spray, the sight of the waves leaping higher, and the sense your vessel is being tossed out of control tends to steal one's total attention.

Add to this, the ongoing thoughts of impending doom. When life throws a difficult situation in your face, it may become difficult to identify the unexpected, as delightful or miraculous as it might be.

A story from the life of Elijah's successor, Elisha, will help illustrate the point. In 2 Kings 6, we read that the King of Aram[34] was engaged in war against Israel. Strangely, the King of Aram realized that the King of Israel always knew his plans in advance. Assuming he had a traitor or spy in his camp, the King of Aram sought to identify the traitor by challenging the troops. They informed him that the prophet Elisha was responsible.

His search for the man of God led him to Dothan where Elisha and his servant were staying. The king's army surrounded the city at night. On the breaking of a new day, the prophet's servant observed the situation and expressed his strong concern. He was afraid! In great confidence, Elisha assured his companion of their safety. Then, in a seemingly automatic gesture, uttered a simple, yet powerful prayer: *"O Lord, I pray, open his eyes that he may see"* (2 Kings 6:17). The petition was answered and the servant saw the mighty hosts of heaven encamped all around them.

All too often we respond in fear rather than faith, as did the servant of Elisha. The realities of the moment can blind us to the spiritual revelations available. For the disciples, the storm clouded their vision and the waves absorbed their energies and focus. In reality, the disciples were not looking for Jesus. No condemnation intended—merely a logical conclusion.

At the risk of stretching the point, I would also suggest this can too easily become a problem in the norms of our lives, apart from the crises and confrontations. For purpose-driven people intent on "taking care of business," this simple reality must be recognized as a potential in daily life. The demands of life, the necessities associated with responsible living, and the desire to succeed, at any level, can absorb our focus as well as our energies. It is not that we are doing anything wrong, we are simply ignoring that which is best.

---

[34] A region northeast of Palestine; currently Syria.

As Jesus made His way to the appointed time for His death on the cross, He stopped at the home of some longtime friends who lived in Bethany. They were two sisters and a brother: Mary, Martha, and Lazarus. Martha assumed the role of gracious hostess and began to fix lunch for their honored guest. She wanted everything to be just right. After all, the privilege of having Jesus in their home was something she never wanted to take for granted, nor did she want to fail in her duty to provide the very best for Him. Mary, on the other hand, sat at the feet of the Lord, listening to every word. Her focus was on hearing Him, not caring for His needs. She focused on enjoying Him—not entertaining Him. We easily detect different mindsets, different personalities, and different engagements. Hear the words Jesus spoke in that setting: *"Martha, Martha, you are worried and bothered about so many things; but only a few things are necessary, really only one, for Mary has chosen the good part, which shall not be taken away from her"* (Luke 10:41, 42). Surely the Lord was not dismissing the necessity of being a good hostess, nor was He dismissing the need to care for those who come to us. He did not criticize Martha for what she was doing, but just spoke a reminder regarding her priorities or her focus. Martha, you're missing the best part.

Every day, it is important to begin with a proper focus. I learned this lesson by way of a personal epiphany 30 years ago. I grew up a Christian—sort of, kind of—and knew that daily devotions were important and "expected." I would read and pray on most days, taking time when it was afforded, but not really practicing a discipline that was consistent. In time, I began to make my devotions a priority and, on occasion, had shared times with my co-workers. I also became aware of my need to have a regular time of exercise as I began to age and my participation in softball, basketball, and other youthful physical endeavors diminished. I began to workout. I would get up early in the morning, head for the gym, and then return home to get ready for the office and have my devotions.

One morning, while lying on the bench preparing for another set of reps with the barbell, I heard the Lord say, "I want to be first in your life." Well, of course! That's the way it should be; that is what is expected of a follower of Christ. Yet, this message was very pointed and very intentional. The Lord was suggesting to me that pumping iron and working out was more important to me than He was. How could He say that? Well, possibly it was the order of my day. I can't say it was a matter of divine jealousy, but I know it was a clarion call to reality. I made a change—from that day on. Sometimes that means I have to get up a little earlier because of scheduled events. That's okay because what I focus on first is what I deem most important—at least that is my sense of it. When I make Jesus the focal point as a normal part of my day, the first part of my day, it is unlikely that I am going to become confused in the times of storm, unable to recognize that He is with me.

From a Kleenex box to a priority of the day, focus remains a simple, yet essential piece. On one occasion recently, as I reached the end of my workout, I stood balanced on a Bosu[35] as I completed my final reps. One lady said, "I don't know many people who can do that." A nearby gentleman simply responded, "It's all about focus." At the risk of over-simplifying life, much of your ability to survive the current crisis or succeed in your life-long calling is the same: focus. When focused correctly, one can develop a rather healthy oblivious-ness.

---

[35] It looks similar to a half ball with a hard platform on the flat side. It is a common piece of equipment in gyms today.

CHAPTER 10

Bonus beyond the Boat

Matthew's Gospel affords an addition to the story not included in the other accounts.[36] Hearing the Master's words, Peter asked the Lord to command him to come to Him on the water. Where did that come from? Yes, Peter was aggressive; in fact, he was impulsive. But, walk on the water? I don't think there had been any conversations, instructions, or encouragements regarding that possibility as a part of the education afforded the twelve in the Lord's school of discipleship.

Far too often, people criticize Peter for his impetuousness and his inability to complete the stroll across the surface of the sea. When Jesus told him to come, he jumped out of the boat and started walking toward Jesus. However, at some point he started to sink and he needed the Lord's intervention. Nevertheless, Peter did walk on water! The list of people claiming this accomplishment is rather short: two, to be exact—Jesus Christ and Simon Peter. We really don't know how far Peter walked before he dropped like a rock. It could have been only a step or two; it could have been a considerable distance. The Scripture provides no indication as to the length of his amble or how far Jesus was from the boat when Peter's adventure began. No matter the distance, the miracle remains.

A simple fact from this phenomenal event in the life of the Apostle Peter stands out, shouting loudly for all to hear. The condition of the sea had threatened Peter and the other disciples to the point of exasperation. The sea had literally become their enemy for much of the previous night. As Peter stepped out of the boat, placing the sole of each foot on the surface of the water, that same sea became the surface upon which he would walk. It is important to note that Peter became fearful due to the wind. In

---

[36] Matthew 14:28-33.

other words, the storm had not totally subsided. The wind had not quit blowing. Peter was stepping out onto a troubled sea. It's one thing to walk on a smooth, stable surface, it's quite another to walk on one that's moving. Whoa! Let's think about this. What a transformation! What a glorious change of circumstances. Peter transitioned from straining at the oars to stepping out of the boat. Furthermore, this miraculous metamorphosis took place in a relatively short span of time. How could this possibly happen?

Peter was, as previously acknowledged, rather impetuous. He ran hot and cold, some might say. A quick glance at his life reflects this reality. Matthew 16:13-23 clearly illustrates his impetuous nature. The famous text describes Jesus blessing Peter for the revelation he has received, but within a matter of moments Peter is being chastised for being an instrument of the devil.

The night before the crucifixion, Jesus met with His disciples. In the midst of the gathering, Peter spoke out with great confidence; some might suggest a bit of bravado: *"Even though all may fall away because of You, I will never fall away"* (Matthew 26:35). As prophesied by the Lord, Peter denied he even knew Jesus—not once, but three times! Was his mouth running before his brain was engaged? Was that the case with his expressed desire to join Jesus on the sea?

Although impulsive, Simon Peter's personality cannot be completely accountable for his dramatic change in this story. Even his previous experiences would not provide a logical explanation for his actions. Though he may have been somewhat daring—a characteristic undoubtedly fostered by his years as a fisherman—there seems to be more at play than propensity. An unusual faith seems to have fueled Peter—a tremendous confidence undergirded him. Without fear, without hesitation, he moved from the comparative safety of the boat to the total vulnerability of the sea. Some people might even label it stupidity. People don't walk on the water.

One simple factor in this story must be emphasized. It was not just Peter's request that enabled the miracle; it was the Lord's response. Jesus said, *"Come"* (Matthew 14:29). No matter how much Peter may have wanted to walk on water, the ability to do so was not within his grasp. This was not a case of mind over matter. Furthermore, faith in faith—as a concept or idea—

will not release the supernatural. Faith is not merely an exercise. Faith is an investment in God. As previously stated, faith means believing God to be who His word declares Him to be and that He can do what He says He will do. Since Jesus said, "Come," Peter was given permission and his faith gave Him the courage and confidence. This experienced fisherman knew very well the likelihood of taking a stroll on the sea, but he decided to do what he had been invited to do: "Come."

How would I respond if the Lord told me to do the impossible? Of course, if Jesus tells someone to do something, it is no longer impossible. A second question must immediately follow: How often have I simply wanted to come to Jesus—to be where He is? You see, Peter did not ask to simply walk on the water, he asked to walk on the water to the Lord. May I suggest a significant difference between wanting to do something purely for the sake of doing it and doing something to be with the Lord.

Forgive me while I leave Peter standing on the water for a few moments to address an associated reality. We will get back to him. I find an interesting addendum to the Lord's encouragement for us to pray. For example, in the passage well-known for its call to prayer, we read: ***"If My people who are called by My name humble themselves and pray, and seek May face and turn from their wicked ways, then I will hear from heaven, will forgive their sin, and will heal their land"*** (2 Chronicles 7:14). In another passage from Jeremiah 29:11-13 we find these familiar words:

> ***"'For I know the plans that I have for you;' declares the Lord, 'plans for welfare and not for calamity to give you a future and a hope. Then you will call upon Me and come and pray to Me, and I will listen to you. And you will seek Me and find Me, when you search for Me with all your heart.'"***

Please note the phrases: "seek My face," and "search for Me with all your heart." It would seem to indicate that God is not just interested in doing things for us. Jesus, being God, the second person of the Trinity, was consistent with the Father. He does not simply want to be the "the butler in the sky." His desire represents much more than provision; He desires relationship with us. Though it may be a stretch, I suggest Peter's success was not the result of his desire to walk on water, but rather his desire to be with the Lord.

At the risk of being redundant, I take you back to a story involving the famed apostle. John 21 gives us the story. Peter, ostensibly bored, frustrated, or something similar, decided to go fishing. Six of the disciples accompanied him on the adventure. They fished all night realizing nothing for their trouble. At the break of day, they saw a figure on the shore who spoke to them. Again, the disciples did not recognize Him. John 21:5 records His words: ***"Children, you do not have any fish, do you?"*** One can only imagine how these grown men felt being referred to as children. Jesus then instructed them to cast their nets on the right side of the boat. Whether they expressed any hesitation or reservation remains unknown, but the disciples followed His advice. In doing so, they realized a phenomenal catch. Peter did not wait for the bounty to be secured. He wrapped his cloak around him and dove into the water, making his way to the shore and the Savior.

Peter was one of the inner circle: Peter, James, and John. It is my opinion that this was a matter of the disciples choosing rather than favoritism shown by the Lord. The three simply pursued a closer relationship with Christ. This same principle applies to our relationship with the Lord today. If we want to know Him more intimately, hear Him more clearly, align ourselves with His desires and plans more consistently, we can do so by pursuing Him more diligently. Don't misunderstand. I do not intend to belittle or demean the other disciples for not being part of the inner circle. Furthermore, no insult or criticism is suggested for their choice to remain in the boat. However, the question arises, "Why did Peter want to walk to where the Lord was— standing on the water—while the other disciples simply sat, staring?" Was it a matter of personality? Was it purely curiosity? Did Peter have an inferiority complex he was trying to massage? Was there some sense of superiority being exhibited, proving a level of spirituality and dynamic faith that surpassed that of his colleagues? Or, is it possible that Peter wanted to be where the Lord was, but not just physically? Could it be the disciple sensed the opportunity to walk in a new realm, experience power, feel elation, and know a level of capability never before considered?

As the fisherman proceeded on his impossible trek, his attention was drawn to his surroundings, and he began to sink. His focus changed. Jesus had not lost His focus, however; it was on Peter. The Scripture reads: ***"Immediately Jesus stretched out His hand and took hold of him, and said to him, 'O you of little faith, why did you doubt?'"*** (Matthew 14:31). I take this to mean: You could have realized your goal, Peter, if you had kept your focus, maintained your faith. The sea did not defeat Peter— his lack of faith brought defeat. Again, no condemnation implied. He did what no one else other than the Lord has done. Yet, he could have walked further; he could have walked all the way to the Lord and possibly with the Lord all the way to shore. Conjecture? I suppose! However, I sometimes wonder what would-a, could-a, should-a been if total faith had been exhibited. That query holds application beyond this moment in Peter's life. I believe it must be applied throughout church history. Personally, I find it significant regarding my own pilgrim journey. What might I have accomplished, what more might I have been able to do, if my faith and my focus had been stronger?

Another aspect of the account needs investigation: ***"Immediately Jesus stretched out His hand and took hold of him."*** So, does that mean Peter had actually walked all the way to where Jesus was, or rather, that Jesus had walked toward Peter as the disciple exercised his faith? Of course, the Lord could have miraculously reached out to Peter from some distance away, but I am inclined to believe He was moving toward the disciple. When we move in obedience and trust, responding to the invitation of our Lord, He will always be there to meet us. My understanding of the Scriptures cause me to believe Jesus and Peter walked back to the boat and boarded. At that point, the wind simply disappeared; calm seas were restored and Peter's spiritual growth took a great step forward. Wet, grateful, and probably still puzzled by what he had just experienced, Peter said nothing. At least, there is nothing recorded in Holy Writ. Was he embarrassed that he had taken his eyes off of Jesus and began to sink? Possibly. Was he elated at the realization that his response to the Lord and his faith in his Master had afforded opportunity to "go where no man has been?" Without a doubt. Though Peter would know failure in the future, he would also become a leader among the disciples helping in the formulation and establishment of the Church. His sermon on the Day of Pentecost, addressed to the crowd that gathered to mock the 120 who were speaking in tongues, still resonates in the Church today. His two epistles have brought comfort, encouragement, and instruction to Christians for two millennia. Could it be that this walk, this step of faith, this impetuous expression created a foundation upon which the ministry of the great apostle was built? Without a doubt, what Peter experienced dramatically impacted his life. Simply stated, what he once feared became the surface upon which he walked.

So, what do you fear? Please understand, I have no desire to judge the legitimacy or fallacy of your fear. Life can be scary. We have all come to recognize our limits and understand the realities of life that are beyond our control. Furthermore, we know the forces of evil and the enemy who threatens and intimidates us. The chosen twelve were of similar cloth and had to deal the realities of life. Peter was not an exceptional individual, yet in the moment, faith surged through his being, he stepped out of the security of the boat, and placed his foot on a surface incapable of supporting him. With the storm still raging and the wind continuing its assault, Peter did the unthinkable. With focus on the Creator, the created performed the impossible. Yes, his doubts would eventually overcome him, but the moment cannot be stripped from his resume. Will you allow the things that threaten you to keep you from knowing the full potential of your walk with God, or will you hear His voice and step out of the boat—even if that step means going beyond the norm and venturing into the unthinkable?

Years ago I discovered a designation on an old map. This replica represented what people once thought the world to be. If memory serves correctly, it appeared in a book—possibly in geography or history class, or it could have been located in an old book opened while exploring the library. The map pictured the world, at least, as it was known at the time. Outside those defined areas lay a rather blank, mystical space that bore the image of a dragon. Wow! That got my attention. I subsequently entitled it, "The Dragon Zone." Explanation from the teacher revealed that this was an unexplored and unknown area. Who knew what might dwell in that region? Possibly dragons or other such creatures lived in that part of the world.

The Dragon Zone has taken on special significance in my life. Beyond using the concept in various sermons and teaching sessions, the Dragon Zone has become an accurate description of some real life experiences. Maps provide a great sense of security. The area is defined, previously explored, and documented. One's level of confidence is dramatically heightened when venturing into new territory with a map in hand. However, there are times in life when we are asked to enter uncharted regions or areas outside our personal experience, knowledge, and comfort. You may recall a reference to the fact that God is more interested in our character than He is our comfort. What are the chances that He would direct our path, at times, into the dragon zone? Despite the uncertainty, the experience and the challenge creates an opportunity to build more than character. It builds trust—trust in Him.

Margaret and I have known the Dragon Zone more than a few times. Growing up in Weed, California, I had the privilege of knowing nearly everyone in town, and I considered every classmate a personal friend. The small town environment provided a safe, stable childhood. Life was good and basically predictable. Consequently, it did not take much to take me outside of my comfort zone. As we left college and launched into ministry, we discovered that nearly every new place took us beyond what we had previously experienced. The summer of 1970 comes to mind as a glowing example.

We had just completed two years in Fallon, Nevada. I had been teaching music in three elementary schools and serving as association pastor of everything. My focus was music, but the church was small and needed leadership in multiple areas. Our daughter, Kristal, was born during that time. Upon sensing it was time to move on, we left the dessert without a place to go. Margaret's parents owned a small restaurant and apartment complex in Colusa, California, so we made our way there, knowing the benefits of family during times of decision and the search for direction. I went back to work for Margaret's brother, Gene, for whom I had worked the first year we were married. I am not sure he really needed my assistance, but he granted me opportunity to work from time to time. I also did small jobs for dad and the neighbors.

After only a short time, I received a phone call from an acquaintance who served as the youth director for the Southern California District of the Assemblies of God. They were planning a summer missions trip to Mexico. Seven Western districts were cooperating in this month long adventure. The person scheduled to provide leadership for the musical expression of the trip had just withdrawn from the assignment. Could I go? Wow! I had been out of college for two years, teaching elementary music, and literally writing or arranging everything the little choir in Fallon had sung during that time. What did I know about leading a choir of 180 high school and college age voices? Some of these young people came from large churches with full-blown music departments. Some of them were music majors in college. Yikes! The Dragon Zone loomed large and imposing. Furthermore, it was way beyond our comfort zone as a family. Todd, our son, was three, and Kristal, our daughter, was only 9 months old when we were scheduled to leave for thirty days. Margaret decided she would go with me, leaving our baby girl in the more than trustworthy arms of Grandma Hill. I still have a hard time believing my wife would make that sacrifice for me.

The trip to Mexico was by train. No, it was not first class. During the journey, I traveled from car to car, introducing music (some of which I had arranged) and trying to become acquainted with the students, especially the musicians. I was blessed: God provided some very talent young people to "make me look good." Amazingly enough, the plan came together and for 30 days, this group of relative strangers from diverse cultures and backgrounds, came together and impacted Mexico City in dramatic fashion. We spent our days on the streets, ministering to people. We spent our nights and free time rehearsing. In the process, unique opportunities were afforded us: a concert in the park drawing more than 25,000 people, a nationally broadcast television appearance, to name a few. Added to this, we had the privilege of coming to know young people who just wanted to do something for God, who wanted to make a difference in our world. It was powerful. Needless to say, it represented one of those moments, one of those experiences that you are simply glad you did not miss. However, from the outset, it took us further into the Dragon Zone than we had ever been.

I take opportunity to mention a few other examples of this reality. As previously mentioned, I became the fifteenth president of Bethany University—its last president, unfortunately. The transition from the pulpit to the academic podium was truly a venture beyond my comfort level. With no stretch of imagination, it was a step out of the boat. However, we had been there before: no, not in the academic arena—in the Dragon Zone.

After our first tenure as lead pastor in Medford, Oregon, we were invited to serve the great church in Albany, Oregon. We had known growth and a tremendous sense of excitement as the church in Medford grew dramatically and continually. How did we do it? I have been asked that many times. I still do not have a good explanation. Suffice it to say, it was God. The church in Albany held a Sunday morning attendance of about 800-900 at the time of our arrival. It had a great history. The previous two pastors were literally icons in our Fellowship: Earl Book and Allen Groff. They had led the church in a growing expression representing the gospel of Jesus Christ locally and around the world. They had also established five daughter churches. Making the move from what I had known to embracing this new challenge was Dragon Zone material.

Over the next 22 plus years, we realized growth in the congregation, the expansion of ministry expressions, acquisition of new properties, and increased influence of the church in our community and the world. At the time of our departure, the church was giving over 30 percent of its income to missions. Needless to say, we had wonderful people, worked with great staff members, and knew the grace and provision of the Lord. It was a great run, and we were continually overwhelmed by God's favor and patience. It was not quite walking on the water but, at times, it seemed an awful lot like it.

Without question, the feeding of the 5,000 left an indelible impression on the disciples. The story was undoubtedly told many times even before it became the official record of Scripture. That kind of miracle does not happen every day. However, the experience that followed—the disciples straining at the oars and the subsequent appearance of Jesus walking through the darkness toward them—creates a picture one simply never wants to forget. But, walking on the water? Well, that was a bonus that Peter and Peter alone would hold and quite possibly harken back to again and again as he moved through the life God had ordained for him. It might be an understatement to label it the Dragon Zone, but the tag would seem appropriate. Peter could have missed it. He could have ignored the opportunity; he could have stayed in the boat. Please understand: staying in the boat is not necessarily a bad thing to do. There were other times in Peter's life when that was exactly what he did. On this particular occasion, however, Jesus said, "Come." Again, at the risk of redundancy, the disciple did not decide to do something crazy on his own. That's not the story. If Peter had stepped out on his own, the only memory would have been that of an embarrassing mistake. This example in Scripture was not preserved to promote recklessness or irresponsibility. However, the call of the Lord still takes place; the wooing of the Spirit can still be heard. If we are open, if we are listening, we may just hear it. When that sound is heard— above the storm, through the darkness and uncertainty of the moment—step out of the boat; invade the Dragon Zone. It is a bonus in life with which nothing else can compare.

CHAPTER 11

Perspective

Life still presents storms, and disciples are still confronted with decisions, difficulties, dilemmas, and disappointments. The Lord still sends His followers into situations that may seem unfair, ill-advised and, at times, even dangerous. Be assured, however, He is not playing games with our lives; He is not being reckless or irresponsible. The Lord has more than proven His love and care for us. We must realize: God is at work. We are privileged to work with Him, to partner with Him for the sake of seeing His plans and desires fulfilled in our world. Truth be known, we may never fully comprehend what it is He is doing. At times, God allows us insight, facilitating a full appreciation of His plan and rejoicing in the thrill of participating in the divine scheme. However, we are not promised that we will always totally understand the process: to whom, how long, and for what purpose. The question should not be, "What is He doing?", but rather, "Am I willing to trust Him and obey Him when I lack understanding and when I feel out of control?"

One of the elements of this story that we can easily overlook or simply underplay is the fact that Jesus came walking toward them on the water. Mark's account states, *"He came to them, walking on the sea; and He intended to pass by them"* (Mark 6:48b). First, note the simple fact that Jesus came to them. He always will. When we respond in faith and assume the role He has given, walk the path He has chosen, embrace the commission He has ushered, we will find Him coming alongside. He has not asked us to do it alone.

My thoughts run to the resurrection of Jesus and the women who had come to the tomb. They were prepared to honor the Lord in the completion of the burial preparation. It was the day after the Sabbath—our Sunday. Mary Magadalene and the other Mary are specifically mentioned in Matthew's Gospel. Introduced to the empty tomb and assured by the angel that Jesus was no longer a resident, the women were instructed to go and tell His disciples the news. The Scripture states, *"And they departed quickly from the tomb with fear and great joy and ran to report it to His disciples"* (Matthew 28:8). They seemed to exhibit incongruous emotions, and yet many people have known the same combination of feelings long after the two women at the tomb. May I suggest that, in serving the Lord, this is how we often find ourselves—obeying His direction and delivering His message with fear and great joy.

Matthew 28:9 provides the ticket, the key, or the assurance we all desperately need: *"And behold Jesus met them and greeted them."* No, He did not wait until they arrived at their destination; He met them on the way. Jesus met the disciples that night on the Sea of Galilee. He met them in the midst of the storm while they were straining at the oars. He came to them, walking on the water. And so it is, and so it always will be. He will come to you; He will not leave you alone. It is His promise; it is His habit. He walks with those who walk His way. He comes alongside those who do His bidding. You may be straining at the oars! It happens. But this is not the time to quit, my friend. Keep your head up; keep your eyes peeled (as my father used to say). You will see Him, I promise. He will come.

Mark's record of the event states, *"He intended to pass them by."* This simple phrase can be troubling, to say the least. Robert A. Guelich offers helpful insight. He states that some interpret the expression as an action that was about to take place: Jesus was about to pass them by. "Others take it to express the disciples' mistaken impression of what Jesus was about to do." Guelich suggests that others understand the wording to mean that Jesus was truly wanting to move past the disciples, possibly to test their faith, or simply because He desired to remain alone.[37]

The Scripture states that the Lord **"came to them."** Possibly this meant the trek across the watery surface had brought Him into some parallel position or in the near vicinity of the disciples.

---

[37] Robert A. Guelich, *Mark 1-8:26*, vol. 34a of *Word Biblical Commentary* (Dallas, TX: Word Books, 1989), 350.

However, if the Lord had no intention of encountering the disciples, why did He walk across the sea, and specifically, take the line of direction that would place Him within view of the twelve? Surely it was possible for Jesus to have taken an alternative route, or even an alternative means of getting to Bethsaida. The fact is, Jesus put himself on a path that placed Him within eyeshot of His devoted followers and, ostensibly, made it more than possible for them to see Him on the water. He wanted them to know He was near. I believe He wanted them to call out to Him, to reach out for His assistance. The disciples, gripped with fear and exhausted from the ordeal, did not recognize the Savior. Rather they expressed fear at the appearance of the One in whom they had come to trust the most. No rebuke was offered for their fear, but rather they knew expressions of understanding and assurance.

Our lives represent interesting moments: times of elation, joy, and celebration; times of relationship, mutually beneficial and memory enhancing. We encounter periods of relaxation, rest, and renewal. We face challenges that stretch us, yet reinforce our sense of confidence in who He has made us to be and what He has enabled us to endure, accomplish, and even conquer. Yet, life can also afford encounters that absorb our total capacity, draining the energy from our bodies, the air from our lungs, and determination from our wills. Within those moments, the Savior comes to us, wherever we may be. Undoubtedly, He intervenes, at times, without delay. Miraculously His presence permeates the atmosphere and His power alters the course of events. At other times, divine intervention seems delayed or withheld, as if for some greater purpose or for some eternal value.

The story of Mary and Martha's desperation caused by the sickness of their brother, Lazarus, comes to mind (John 11). Though word was sent to the Healer, He delayed His departure, arriving on the scene after the afflicted had died. No failure occurred, however, though the sisters of the deceased understood it to be the case. Jesus had something greater in mind; a demonstration of His power over death itself was scheduled for Bethany. Without doubt, healing was needed and the expectations of the sisters for a resolution to the illness endured by Lazarus existed. However, resurrection from the dead and the restoration of life sent a message far beyond the immediate family and the limits of the little village. Simply said, God had a better idea.

Was it possible for the disciples' trip across the Sea of Galilee to be made effortlessly, without mishap, or delay? Surely, we know it's true. Could Jesus have calmed the storm before the disciples ever caught a glimpse of Him? Without question! Yet, that was not the plan. Would the chosen twelve ever fully know all that was being accomplished through their "straining at the oars"? It would seem impossible to say. In faith, they obeyed the instruction of the Lord. In faith, they proceeded against the resistance of the sea and the atmosphere. Because of their faith, Jesus would not allow them to go it alone. He showed up!

The word "faith" fluidly flows from the lips of Christians, but the actual realization of the concept seems to only become apparent in the hard places and scary situations. To stand tall and talk of His goodness when the bills are current, the children behave, and the sun shines for the entire vacation takes little effort. However, when the storm rages, our craft is threatened, the sky appears black, the eerie sound of the enemy's laughter seems to ride on the wind, and confession of our confidence may come reluctantly. Yet, an expression of faith in that moment rings of something far beyond the expected. It is there, in that place, that the validity and the true value of faith is revealed.

Our faith will be tested. God does not need to validate the legitimacy of our faith. He knows exactly the strength or weakness of our trust in Him. He wants us to realize the true "condition" of our faith. Just because we utter a confession does not mean that we have experienced the true essence of faith.

Obviously, faith is the currency with which we acquire salvation. The Apostle Paul wrote: ***"For by grace you have been saved through faith; and that not of yourselves, it is the gift of God; not as a result of works, so that no one may boast"*** (Ephesians 2:8, 9). Grace is provided by the Father, demonstrated through the provision of His Son, Jesus Christ, who was sent to die as the perfect Lamb for the forgiveness of sin. Faith is the investment required on our part to realize that provision. Too often, however, confession represents the only expression of one's faith. Romans 10:9, 10 tells us that if we make confession with our mouth and have belief in our heart, we will be saved. The belief in the heart is a critical piece. Speaking it is one thing; embracing it with conviction is quite another. Josh McDowell and Bob Hostetler address this matter in their book, *Beyond Beliefs to Convictions*: "Today merely 'believing' isn't enough. Not because believing isn't important; it is. But ... in today's culture believing is made out to be more of a preference based on one's subjective feelings at the moment. And that kind of believing isn't enough."[38] Beliefs can become a matter of convenience. In a given setting, among a select group of people, one can simply confess the accepted norm—be that political, social, or theological. In fact, many people may well feel a pressure to confess the accepted norm. The desire for acceptance and approval can easily translate into the recital of the majority opinion. Conviction, however, is what I would equate to the "belief in the heart" piece of the equation given in Paul's letter to the Romans. McDowell and Hostetler lend valuable insight: "To have *convictions* is to be thoroughly convinced that something is true—'the state of being convinced of error or compelled to admit the truth.'"[39] This moves one beyond feelings, beyond peer pressure, beyond the recital of creeds or liturgy. Conviction, a deep seated and totally persuaded willingness to base not only my decisions, but also my life on what I believe, legitimizes my confession.

Confession backed with conviction is the kind of faith that sends you across the sea when you are not sure why you are going. It is the kind of faith that keeps you rowing when the storm is raging and makes you willing to step out of the boat simply because the Savior has invited you to "come." This kind of faith releases the miraculous.

Some people suggest that the world awaits an expression of true Christianity. I remember hearing one of my high school teachers say, "No one knows if Christianity is for real because no one has ever met a real Christian," or something to that effect. The statement, supposedly a quote from a respected person of the day, has haunted me since. Could it be that my life has creat-

---

[38] Josh McDowell and Bob Hostetler, *Beyond Beliefs to Convictions* (Wheaton, IL: Tyndale House, 2002), 21.

[39] Ibid., 22.

ed doubt rather than affirmed the reality of Christ and validated faith in Him? Multiple examples of true Christianity can be found throughout church history, discounting the claim of the originator of the above supposition. However, do the people in my world tend to believe or disbelieve in Christ based on the actions, attitudes, and associations they experience in me? It is not enough to discount their opinion because they do not understand or have become confused by social commentary. The call to be light and salt still resonates in the ear of every true believer. The darkest place provides opportunity for light to shine the brightest. The blandness and rottenness of life validates the need for salt. Are we up to the task? Will we respond to the Master—even when tired, frustrated, or lack understanding? Is our faith a mere confession or is it a deep seated conviction that embraces the opportunity to walk on water?

Keep in mind that without the storm, we have no story. Another casual voyage across the Sea of Galilee is only another detail in the Gospel record that may not even be worthy of inclusion in Holy Writ. And yet, here it is, garnering attention, study, and appreciation. People have learned lessons, recognized principles, revealed truth, and influenced lives far beyond the limits of those directly involved or even the generation in which they lived. Eternal impact has been realized. Wow! How quickly we can deduce that God has failed, that we, as disciples, have made a mistake, that the devil is winning, that our faith is invalid. Oh, awaken, my friend. Open your eyes and your heart to the screening of the whole movie. Never become satisfied with the possession of a snapshot. God is always at work, doing far more than we understand, accomplishing much more than we can appreciate, and yielding more than is measurable within the moment.

Trust and obey, for there's no other way,
To be happy in Jesus, but to trust and obey.[40]

So, row on, my friend, row on! It is not time for you to quit, nor is it time for you to lay down your oars. I suggest, however, that you turn, from time to time, and take a look. Above the surf,

---

[40] John H. Sammis, "Trust and Obey," hymn, 1887.

91

beyond the wind, you will see Him—He is coming. Before you know it, you will be standing on the other side, side-by-side with Him.

ABOUT THE AUTHOR

Lewis Shelton has been a musician, pastor, teacher, professor, and college president. His current focus on writing is the next phase of his life's journey. He lives with his wife, Margaret, in the beautiful state of Oregon, and enjoys golf, fishing, his family, and opportunities to speak. He holds a doctor of ministry degree and an honorary doctorate. His interest in leadership and desire to help develop the same opens doors for mentoring, which he thoroughly enjoys.

88900747R00057

Made in the USA
Middletown, DE
13 September 2018